RELIABLE
MESSENGERS

FROM PASSIVE TO PURPOSEFUL IN ONE YEAR

ISBN: 979-8-9944908-0-8

First published 2026

TABLE OF CONTENTS

A WORD ABOUT YOUR JOURNEY

This is intentionally designed as a 52-week field guide, not a 365-day devotional—and that choice matters. I've learned that daily devotionals, while valuable, can quickly become overwhelming. When you miss a day (and life happens), guilt often follows, and before long, the guide sits on a shelf collecting dust instead of transforming your life.

I designed this differently on purpose.

Each week focuses on one significant concept or biblical truth—something substantial enough to warrant your full attention. Here's how to get the most from this journey:

Day 1: Read the week's entry thoughtfully. Take your time. Let the stories, Scripture, and teaching sink in deeply.

Days 2-7: Engage with the "Living It Out" section. These aren't optional extras—they're where transformation happens. Use the reflection questions for journaling or discussion. Take on the weekly challenge. Try the implementation suggestions. Let the Holy Spirit work the truth from your head into your heart and hands.

The rhythm of focused reading followed by six days of practical application will move you from information to transformation. It gives the Holy Spirit room to work. It respects the reality of your life while challenging you toward genuine growth.

Don't rush ahead. Don't try to do more than one week at a time. Trust the process. Some weeks will speak more directly to your current season than others, and that's exactly as it should be.

Enjoy the journey—one week at a time!

A Note About the Stories in This Book

Throughout this 52-week journey, each week begins with a story designed to illuminate the biblical principle we're exploring. These opening narratives fall into three categories:

Historical Accounts: These are documented events from history, such as Ruby Bridges integrating schools in 1960, Martin Luther nailing his 95 Theses to the church door, or Churchill's leadership during World War II. Where possible, I've provided citations for further reading about these remarkable true stories.

Stories Inspired by True Events: Some narratives are based on historical events but include reconstructed dialogue, thoughts, or details that help illustrate the spiritual principle. For example, while the Wright Brothers did pioneer flight and later taught others, the specific conversations are representative rather than documented.

Teaching Illustrations: Some stories serve as modern parables—narratives or teaching tools designed to help you grasp spiritual concepts. Like Jesus' parables, their power lies not in their historical documentation but in their ability to communicate truth.

I've chosen this approach because reliable messengers throughout history have used stories to communicate God's truth—sometimes historical accounts, sometimes parables, always with the goal of transformation rather than just information. As you read each week's opening story, focus less on the category it falls into and more on the truth it's designed to convey about becoming a reliable messenger of God's grace.

INTRODUCTION

In a world drowning in information but starving for truth, God is calling His people to be reliable messengers. This comprehensive 52-week guide will transform you from a passive observer to an active participant in God's mission, equipping you with the biblical foundation, practical tools, and spiritual framework necessary to represent Christ effectively in every sphere of your influence.

This book is based on the foundational truth of Proverbs 13:17 (NLT)—"An unreliable messenger stumbles into trouble, but a reliable messenger brings healing." Think of this as a field guide that will lead you through a systematic exploration of what it means to be God's reliable messenger in the 21st century. Here's what I've discovered: reliable messengers aren't born but made through intentional development, biblical understanding, and faithful practice.

The journey ahead is both challenging and rewarding. Over the next year, you'll be guided through four crucial paradigm shifts that separate reliable messengers from ordinary believers: moving from anchors to oars (from passive to active engagement), from cruise ship to fishing boat mentality (from comfort-seeking to mission-focused), from fear to freedom (from paralysis to bold faith), and from parishioner to practitioner (from consumer to contributor). Each shift builds upon the others, creating a comprehensive transformation in how you understand your role in God's kingdom.

This guide is structured around proven frameworks that have developed effective messengers throughout church history. You'll explore the E5 process (Encounter, Experience, Exchange, Endeavor, Encouragement) that shows how God transforms ordinary people into extraordinary servants. You'll master the E4 leadership model (Engage, Equip, Empower, Encourage) that multiplies your influence through others. You'll learn the E3 communication principles (Explicit, Explainable, Essential) that make your message clear and compelling.

More than theoretical knowledge, this guide provides practical application in partnership with your local church's Mission, Vision, Values, and Strategies (MVVS) framework. You'll discover how to GATHER consistently for community and encouragement, GROW intentionally through discipleship that multiplies, and GO strategically to serve both local and global needs. The T4 stewardship model will teach you to invest your Time, Talents, Treasures, and Testimony for maximum kingdom impact.

Each week's content is designed to be both substantive and accessible, requiring approximately 15 minutes of focused engagement. But let me be clear—this isn't passive reading. It's interactive learning. Every chapter includes reflection questions that help you personalize the content, weekly challenges that move you from theory to practice, and implementation suggestions that create lasting change in your daily life.

The biblical examples throughout this guide aren't just historical accounts—they're practical models for your own development. You'll learn from reliable messengers like Elijah's courage to stand alone for truth, Abraham's willingness to step out in faith, Moses' transformation from reluctant servant to faithful leader, and Paul's radical exchange of worldly success for kingdom impact. You'll also learn from negative examples, understanding what makes messengers unreliable and how to avoid those pitfalls.

Whether you're a new believer discovering your calling for the first time, a mature Christian seeking to increase your effectiveness, a church leader wanting to develop others, or someone who feels inadequate for God's purposes, this guide meets you where you are and takes you where God wants you to be.

The ultimate goal isn't just personal spiritual growth—though that will certainly happen. The goal is transformation into a reliable messenger who experiences and demonstrates the extraordinary life Jesus promised in John 10:10. This abundant life isn't found in perfect circumstances but in the perfect presence of Christ transforming ordinary circumstances through willing messengers.

As you begin this journey, remember that becoming a reliable messenger is both a destination and a process. You'll never "arrive" at perfect reliability, but you can continuously grow in faithfulness, effectiveness, and impact. The principles you'll learn aren't just for this year—they're for a lifetime of faithful service.

The world desperately needs what you'll become through this process: reliable messengers who can bridge the gap between divine truth and human need, who can translate eternal principles into practical application, and who can demonstrate through their lives that following Christ leads to genuine transformation and abundant living.

Your journey as a reliable messenger begins now. Step forward with confidence, knowing that the same God who called and equipped messengers throughout Scripture is calling and equipping you for this vital role in His eternal purposes.

QUARTER 1
FOUNDATIONS OF RELIABLE MESSAGING

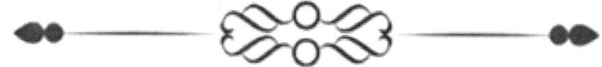

Understanding Our Calling and Identity (Weeks 1-13)

WEEK 1

WHAT MAKES A MESSENGER RELIABLE?

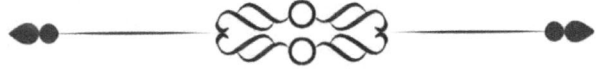

Proverbs 13:17 (NLT) - An unreliable messenger stumbles into trouble, but a reliable messenger brings healing.

In 1960, a young African American girl named Ruby Bridges walked through angry crowds to attend an all-white elementary school in New Orleans. At just six years old, she became a reliable messenger of change, her quiet courage speaking louder than any words. What made her reliable wasn't her age or her eloquence—it was her faithfulness to the mission entrusted to her.

The Hebrew word for "reliable" in Proverbs 13:17 is *ne'eman*, meaning faithful, trustworthy, or established. It's the same word used to describe God's faithfulness throughout Scripture. When Solomon contrasts the "wicked messenger" with the "trustworthy envoy," he's revealing a fundamental truth: the character of the messenger determines the effectiveness of the message.

A reliable messenger in biblical terms possesses three essential qualities: faithfulness (unwavering commitment to the message), integrity (alignment between character and calling), and competence (adequate preparation and skill). These aren't natural talents we're born with—they're spiritual qualities developed through relationship with God.

Consider the difference between a wicked messenger and a reliable one. The wicked messenger "falls into trouble"—why? Because they distort the message for personal gain, deliver it carelessly, or abandon their post when difficulty comes. But the reliable messenger "brings healing"—their very presence becomes therapeutic to those around them.

In our digital age, we're all messengers. Every social media post, every conversation, every action sends a message about what we believe and whom we serve. The question isn't whether we're messengers—it's whether we're reliable ones.

Here's what I've found encouraging: God isn't looking for perfect messengers; He's looking for faithful ones. Moses had a speech impediment, yet God used him to deliver the Israelites. David was a shepherd boy, yet God chose him to lead a nation. Mary was a teenage girl from a small town, yet God selected her to bring the Messiah into the world.

What makes you reliable isn't your background, education, or natural ability. It's your willingness to faithfully carry the message God has entrusted to you, regardless of the cost or the opposition you may face.

Living It Out

Reflection Questions:

1. What messages are you currently carrying in your life, work, and relationships?

2. How does your character align with the messages you're sending?

3. What areas of your life need greater faithfulness to become a more reliable messenger?

Weekly Challenge: Identify one relationship where you can be a "healing" presence this week. Practice being reliable in small things—return phone calls promptly, keep commitments, speak truthfully even when it's difficult.

Implementation Ideas:

- Start each day by asking God to make you a reliable messenger.

- Keep a journal of opportunities to represent Christ well.

- Find an accountability partner to help you grow more reliable.

- Study the character qualities of biblical messengers you admire.

WEEK 2

CALLED TO CARRY THE MESSAGE

Isaiah 6:8-9 (ESV) - And I heard the voice of the Lord saying, "Whom shall I send, and who will go for us?" Then I said, "Here I am! Send me." And he said, "Go, and say to this people: 'Keep on hearing, but do not understand; keep on seeing, but do not perceive.'

The year was 1940, and Gladys Aylward, a former housemaid from London, found herself leading 100 Chinese orphans on a treacherous journey across mountains to safety during the Japanese invasion. She had no formal training, no financial backing, and no political connections. What she had was a clear calling and unshakeable faith that God had appointed her as His messenger to the people of China.

In Isaiah chapter 6, Isaiah's calling experience in the temple reveals the process by which God calls ordinary people to be His messengers. First came the vision—Isaiah saw the Lord "high and lifted up." Then came conviction—"Woe is me, for I am undone!" Next came cleansing—the angel touched his lips with a coal from the altar. Finally came the commissioning— "Whom shall I send, and who will go for us?"

Notice something remarkable here: God didn't ask Isaiah specifically. He asked generally, "Whom shall I send?" This suggests that God's call often comes as an invitation rather than a command. He's looking for volunteers, not conscripts. He wants willing hearts, not reluctant servants.

Isaiah's response—"Here I am! Send me"—contains three powerful elements. "Here am I" speaks of availability. "Send me" speaks of accountability. And that exclamation point? It speaks of eagerness. This wasn't a resigned "I guess I'll go if I have to." This was enthusiastic "I can't wait to represent You!"

But God's response to Isaiah is sobering. He essentially says, "Go, but know that many won't listen. Some will hear but not understand. Others will see but not perceive." God was honest about the challenges Isaiah would face as His messenger. The calling was clear, but it wouldn't be easy.

This is crucial for us to understand. Being called as God's messenger doesn't guarantee success as the world defines it. It doesn't promise popularity, prosperity, or ease of life. What it promises is purpose, God's presence, and the assurance that our lives matter in His eternal plan. It doesn't get better than that!

Every believer has been called to be God's messenger. The Great Commission isn't just for pastors, church staff, and missionaries—it's for every follower of Christ. You may not be called to preach from a pulpit or serve in a foreign country, but you are called to represent Christ wherever you are.

Your workplace needs a reliable messenger of God's integrity. Your neighborhood needs a reliable messenger of God's love. Your family needs a reliable messenger of God's grace. The question isn't whether you're called—it's whether you're willing to say, "Here I am! Send me."

Like Gladys Aylward leading those children to safety, you may not feel qualified for the mission God has for you. But here's the truth: qualification isn't the issue—availability is. God doesn't call those who have been fully equipped; He fully equips those He calls.

Living It Out

Reflection Questions:

1. When have you experienced a clear sense of God's calling in your life?

2. What fears or feelings of inadequacy keep you from fully embracing your role as God's messenger?

3. Where is God currently asking you to represent Him, even if it feels beyond your comfort zone?

Weekly Challenge: Practice saying "Here I am, send me" in small situations this week. When you see a need, respond with availability before calculating the cost. Look for three opportunities to represent Christ where you might normally stay silent or invisible.

Implementation Ideas:

- Study other biblical callings (Moses, Gideon, Mary, Paul) and note the patterns.

- Write out your personal "Here I am, send me" prayer and pray it daily.

- Identify three specific places where God might be calling you to be His messenger.

- Share your sense of calling with a trusted friend or mentor for accountability.

WEEK 3

EQUIPPED FOR THE MISSION

2 Timothy 2:2 (NLT) - You have heard me teach things that have been confirmed by many reliable witnesses. Now teach these truths to other trustworthy people who will be able to pass them on to others.

During World War II, a young seminary student named Dietrich Bonhoeffer could have stayed safely in America, pursuing his academic career. Instead, he returned to Nazi Germany, convinced that he needed to be equipped not just with theological knowledge but with the courage to live faithfully under pressure. His commitment to faithfully passing on the gospel cost him his life, but his influence continues to equip reliable messengers decades later.

Paul's words to Timothy reveal God's strategy for building reliable messengers: multiplication through faithful transmission. Notice the four generations Paul envisions: Paul → Timothy → faithful men → others also. This isn't a game of theological telephone where the message gets distorted with each step and person. This is intentional discipleship where reliable messengers carefully preserve and pass on the essential truths of the faith.

The word "commit" here means to entrust or deposit for safekeeping—like placing valuable items in a bank vault. Paul's declaration shows us that equipping reliable messengers requires three essential elements.

First, there's **content** (what to pass on). Paul specifically mentions "things that have been confirmed by many reliable witnesses"—not everything Paul ever said, but the essential gospel truths that must be preserved unchanged. Today, this content is found in Scripture—the complete revelation of God's truth that equips us for every good work.

Second, we need **character** (who can be trusted with it). Paul specifies "trustworthy people"—those whose reliability has been proven over time. Here's what I've observed: faithfulness matters more than natural talent. God can use someone with limited ability but proven character far more than someone with great gifts but questionable faithfulness.

Finally, there's **competence** (the ability to teach others). The phrase "who will be able to pass them on to others" indicates that being equipped isn't just about personal knowledge—it's about the capacity to reproduce that knowledge in others.

The beauty of Paul's model is its sustainability. Instead of trying to personally disciple everyone, Paul equipped key leaders who could equip others, who could equip others. This multiplication principle and process allows the gospel to spread exponentially rather than just additively.

Here is what this requires of us: we must be both good students and good teachers. We need to receive faithfully from those who've gone before us, and we need to give faithfully to those coming after us. We're links in a chain that stretches back to the apostles and forward to future generations.

Consider the people who equipped you in your faith journey. Perhaps it was a parent who read you Bible stories, a Bible study leader who showed you how to apply Scripture, a mentor who modeled Christian living, or a pastor who challenged you to grow. You are part of their spiritual legacy.

Consider this: who are you equipping? Who is receiving from you the truths that have shaped your life? God hasn't equipped you just for your own benefit—He's equipped you to equip others.

Living It Out

Reflection Questions:

1. Who has been the key "Pauls" in your life—people who equipped you in your faith?

2. What essential truths have you received that you need to faithfully pass on to others?

3. Who are the potential "Timothys" in your life—people you could invest in and equip?

Weekly Challenge: Identify one person you can begin intentionally equipping this week. Start with something simple—share a meaningful Scripture verse, recommend a helpful book, or invite them to discuss a spiritual topic over coffee.

Implementation Ideas:

- List the most important spiritual truths you've learned and consider how to share them.

- Develop a simple framework for sharing your faith story with others.

- Look for natural mentoring opportunities in your current relationships.

- Consider joining or starting a discipleship group focused on multiplication.

WEEK 4

THE MESSENGER'S REFRESHING POWER

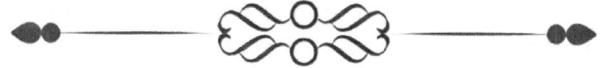

Proverbs 25:13 (ESV) - Like the cold of snow in the time of harvest is a faithful messenger to those who send him; he refreshes the soul of his masters.

(Teaching Illustration) In the scorching heat of California's Central Valley, workers labor through summer days that can reach 110 degrees. When a supervisor arrives with ice-cold water, the relief is immediate and profound. The workers don't just receive hydration—they receive hope, energy, and the strength to continue. This simple act of refreshment can mean the difference between despair and perseverance.

Solomon's comparison in Proverbs 25:13 would have resonated powerfully with his original audience. Palestine's harvest season occurred during the hottest, driest months of the year. The idea of "cold snow" during harvest time would have seemed impossible—except in the high mountains where snow remained year-round. Messengers would sometimes retrieve this precious snow to bring refreshment to harvest workers below.

The Hebrew word for "refreshes" is *yashib*, which means to restore, revive, or bring back to life. A reliable messenger doesn't just deliver information—they bring restoration to weary souls. They arrive like a cold drink on a sweltering day, providing exactly what's needed when it's needed most.

But here's something beautiful: notice the reciprocal nature of this refreshment. The messenger refreshes "the soul of his masters"—those who sent him. When we serve as reliable messengers for God, we bring refreshment not only to those who receive the message but also joy to the heart of God who sent us. Our faithfulness delights the Father.

Think about the people in your life who have been "snow in the time of harvest" to you. Maybe it was a friend who called just when you needed encouragement, or a coworker who offered help during a crisis, or even a family member who believed in you when you couldn't believe in yourself. These people understood that being a reliable messenger isn't just about grand gestures—it's about bringing God's refreshment to everyday situations.

The power to refresh others comes from several sources. There's **timing**—reliable messengers have developed sensitivity to God's Spirit and to the needs of others. There's **content**—the refreshment they bring isn't empty positivity but substantive hope rooted in God's truth. There's **character**—their reliability itself becomes a source of refreshment in a world full of broken promises. And there's **perspective**—they help others see their situations from God's eternal viewpoint.

Consider Jesus, the ultimate reliable messenger. Everywhere He went, He brought refreshment to weary souls. The woman at the well received living water. The disciples received rest when He calmed the storm. The mourners received comfort when He raised Lazarus. Even today, His words continue to refresh millions around the world.

As His representatives, we carry this same refreshing power. When we speak truth with love, offer help without expectation, or simply show up when others need us, we become instruments of God's refreshment in a world that's desperately thirsty.

Living It Out

Reflection Questions:

1. Who in your life has been like "cold snow in the time of harvest" to you?

2. How can you develop greater sensitivity to recognize when others need refreshment?

3. What specific refreshment do you have to offer others based on your experiences with God?

Weekly Challenge: Be intentionally refreshing to three different people this week. Look for those who seem weary, discouraged, or overwhelmed. Offer the specific type of encouragement or help that would be most meaningful to them.

Implementation Ideas:

- Keep a list of encouraging Scripture verses to share with others.

- Develop the habit of asking people, "How can I pray for you?"

- Look for practical ways to serve others (bring meals, offer rides, help with projects).

- Practice the ministry of presence—sometimes just being available is the greatest refreshment.

WEEK 5

FROM PARISHIONER TO PRACTITIONER

James 1:22-25 (AMP) - But prove yourselves doers of the word [actively and continually obeying God's precepts], and not merely listeners [who hear the word but fail to internalize its meaning], deluding yourselves [by unsound reasoning contrary to the truth]. For if anyone only listens to the word without obeying it, he is like a man who looks very carefully at his natural face in a mirror; for once he has looked at himself and gone away, he immediately forgets what he looked like. But he who looks carefully into the perfect law, the law of liberty, and faithfully abides by it, not having become a [careless] listener who forgets but an active doer [who obeys], he will be blessed and favored by God in what he does [in his life of obedience].

Teaching Illustration) Maria had attended church faithfully for fifteen years. She knew the order of service, sang the hymns, and took notes during sermons. She was the picture of a good church member—until the day her pastor challenged the people to move beyond consumption to contribution. That challenge launched Maria into a journey from the building to the community, where she discovered that being a reliable messenger meant more than just receiving God's Word—it meant doing it.

James uses a powerful analogy to illustrate the difference between hearing and doing. He compares someone who hears God's Word but doesn't act on it to a person who looks in a mirror, sees what needs to be fixed, but walks away and immediately forgets what they saw. It's absurd when you think about it, yet this describes the spiritual condition of many believers.

The word "doers" in Greek is *poietes*, from which we get our English word "poet." A poet doesn't just read words—they create them. Similarly, a doer of God's Word doesn't just consume spiritual content—they create spiritual reality through their obedience.

James contrasts two types of people. There's the **careless listener**—someone who engages with God's Word intellectually but fails to let it transform their behavior. They might be Bible scholars who can discuss theology for hours but whose lives don't reflect the love they study.

Then there's the **active doer**—someone who looks intently into God's Word (the "perfect law of liberty") and continues in it. The word "continues" suggests persistence and consistency. This person doesn't just have momentary spiritual highs—they develop lifestyle patterns that reflect God's truth.

The shift from parishioner to practitioner represents one of the most crucial paradigm changes in spiritual growth. A parishioner's primary relationship to the church is receiving—receiving teaching, receiving ministry, receiving comfort. While receiving is important, it was never intended to be the end goal.

A practitioner, on the other hand, sees themselves as an active participant in God's mission. They ask different questions. Instead of "What can I get?" they ask "What can I give?" Instead of "How can the church serve me?" they ask

"How can I serve through the church?" Instead of "What's wrong with the message?" they ask "How can I apply this message?"

This doesn't mean practitioners are more spiritual or valuable than others. It means they've recognized that spiritual maturity involves moving from dependence to interdependence, from consumption to contribution.

Take the disciples' transformation. Initially, they were followers who received Jesus' teaching. But after Pentecost, they became practitioners who put that teaching into action. Peter, who once denied Christ, became a bold preacher. John, who wanted to call down fire on the Samaritans, became known as the apostle of love.

Here's what I've learned: the beauty of becoming a practitioner is that it doesn't require perfection—it requires participation. You don't have to have all the answers to start applying what you know. You don't have to be a theological expert to begin serving others.

Living It Out

Reflection Questions:

1. In what areas of your spiritual life are you more of a consumer than a contributor?
2. What specific truth from God's Word have you been hearing but not fully practicing?
3. How could you move from receiving ministry to providing ministry in your current circumstances?

Weekly Challenge: Choose one area where you've been a "forgetful hearer" and take specific action to become a "blessed doer." Whether it's forgiveness, generosity, evangelism, or service, move from theory to practice.

Implementation Ideas:

- After reading Scripture or hearing a sermon, always ask "What should I do differently?"

- Find ways to serve in your church or community based on your gifts and interests.

- Look for opportunities to share what you've learned with others.

- Set up accountability to help you follow through on spiritual commitments.

WEEK 6

ANCHORS TO OARS: GETTING IN THE GAME

Luke 5:1-11 (ESV) - Getting into one of the boats, which was Simon's, he asked him to put out a little from the land... And when he had finished speaking, he said to Simon, "Put out into the deep and let down your nets for a catch."

In 1961, President John F. Kennedy announced an audacious goal: America would land a man on the moon before the decade ended. At the time, the United States was losing the space race to the Soviet Union. Many experts said it was impossible—the technology didn't exist, the risks were enormous, and the costs were astronomical. The safe approach would have been to continue incremental improvements to existing programs. Instead, Kennedy challenged the nation to stop being anchored to what seemed possible and start rowing toward what seemed impossible. Eight years later, Neil Armstrong stepped onto the lunar surface. The difference between failure and success wasn't better technology or more money—it was the decision to move from anchor thinking to oar thinking, from playing it safe to pursuing an audacious goal.

In Luke 5, the fishing boat rocked gently in the shallow water as Peter and his companions cleaned their nets after a frustrating night. They had worked hard, yet they caught nothing. They were ready to anchor their boat and call it a day.

Then Jesus stepped into their boat and changed everything—not just their fishing success, but their entire approach to life. He taught them the difference between being an anchor that holds things in place and being an oar that moves things forward.

When Peter and his partners were anchored to their previous night's failure, Jesus invited them to push out into deeper waters and try again. Their willingness to move from anchor thinking to active obedience resulted in a catch so large it nearly sank two boats.

An **anchor mindset** focuses on security, stability, and staying put. While anchors serve an important purpose—providing stability during storms—they also prevent movement and progress. In the church, people with anchor mentalities often say things like: "We've never done it that way before," "Let's wait and see what happens," or "Someone else should handle that."

An **oar mindset,** by contrast, focuses on movement, progress, and active participation. People with oar mentalities say: "How can I help make this happen?" "What's the next step we should take?" "Let's try something new."

Notice what happened when Peter shifted from anchor to oar thinking. First, he had to trust Jesus despite his expertise. As a professional fisherman, Peter knew that daytime fishing in those waters was unlikely to produce results. But he said, "But at your word I will let down the nets." His willingness to act despite his doubts opened the door to miraculous provision.

Second, Peter had to involve others. The catch was so large that he called for help from his partners. Here's an important truth: God's best work often requires community effort. When we move from anchor to oar thinking, we discover that we need each other to accomplish what God has in mind.

Third, Peter experienced transformation through action. The miracle didn't happen when Peter discussed fishing with Jesus—it happened when Peter actually let down the nets. Many people spend more time talking about what they should do than actually doing it. Reliable messengers understand that transformation comes through obedience, not just understanding.

The result of Peter's paradigm shift was life-altering. Jesus told him, "From now on you will catch men." Peter went from catching fish for a living to catching people for the kingdom. But this transformation required him to "forsake all and follow"—to completely abandon his anchor mentality and embrace an oar lifestyle.

Consider your own approach to spiritual growth and ministry. Are you anchored to familiar routines, comfortable relationships, and safe environments? Or are you willing to pick up oars and venture into deeper waters where God might do something unexpected?

Being a reliable messenger requires oar thinking. It means being willing to move when God says move, even when you can't see the destination. It means participating actively in God's work rather than just observing from a safe distance.

Living It Out

Reflection Questions:

1. In what areas of your life are you currently "anchored" when God might be calling you to take up "oars"?

2. What fears or past disappointments keep you from venturing into deeper waters with God?

3. How might God want to use your willingness to "let down the nets" to bless others?

Weekly Challenge: Identify one area where you've been playing it safe and take a specific step of faith this week. Whether it's starting a difficult conversation, volunteering for a new responsibility, or reaching out to someone you've been meaning to contact, move from anchor to oar.

Implementation Ideas:

- List three areas where you've been passive and brainstorm active steps you could take.

- Find a mentor or accountability partner who will encourage you to take godly risks.

- Pray specifically for courage to obey God even when His direction doesn't make logical sense.

- Study other biblical examples of people who moved from safety to faith-filled action.

WEEK 7

CRUISE SHIP VS. FISHING BOAT MENTALITY

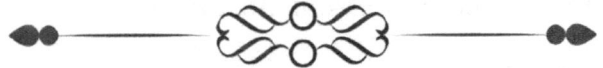

Matthew 4:18-22 (NLT) - One day as Jesus was walking along the shore of the Sea of Galilee, he saw two brothers—Simon, also called Peter, and Andrew—throwing a net into the water, for they fished for a living. Jesus called out to them, "Come, follow me, and I will show you how to fish for people!"

(Story Inspired by True Events) In 1912, the RMS Titanic set sail on its maiden voyage as the ultimate luxury cruise ship. Everything was designed for passenger comfort and entertainment—elegant dining rooms, a grand staircase, a swimming pool, and even a gymnasium. The ship's motto could have been "Your comfort is our priority." Meanwhile, across the Atlantic, small fishing boats left port each day with one simple purpose: to catch fish. These boats had no luxurious amenities, no entertainment staff, and no focus on passenger comfort. Every decision was made based on one question: "Will this help us catch more fish?"

The contrast couldn't be more striking. On one side, a massive cruise ship with every amenity imaginable. On the other side, a simple fishing boat with nets, basic equipment, and a crew focused on one thing: catching fish. Both are valid vessels, but they serve completely different purposes. One exists for the comfort of those on board; the other exists to accomplish a mission.

When Jesus called Peter and Andrew, they were in a fishing boat doing what fishing boats do—seeking fish. Jesus' invitation, "Follow Me, and I will make you fishers of men," wasn't asking them to abandon their work ethic or sense of purpose. He was expanding their mission from catching fish to catching people for God's kingdom.

Unfortunately—and here's where it gets personal—many modern churches have unintentionally shifted from a fishing boat mentality to a cruise ship mentality. The cruise ship church focuses primarily on the comfort, entertainment, and satisfaction of those already on board. Success is measured by how happy the passengers are, how smooth the ride is, and how many amenities are available.

The fishing boat church, by contrast, focuses primarily on the mission of reaching those not yet on board. While they care deeply about those in the boat, their primary energy goes toward the work of fishing. Success is measured by how many fish are caught, how effectively the crew works together, and how well they navigate to where the fish are.

Consider the characteristics of each mentality. **Cruise ship churches** have an inward focus (those already aboard), comfort as the primary goal, and professional staff doing the work while passengers relax. **Fishing boat churches** have an outward focus (the fish not yet caught), mission as the primary goal, and everyone on board having a role in the fishing.

Jesus was clear about the church's primary purpose. In the Great Commission, He told His followers to "go and make disciples." That's fishing boat language. The early church understood this—they devoted themselves to prayer, teaching, fellowship, and breaking bread, but always with an outward

29

focus on reaching others.

Now, this doesn't mean cruise ship elements are wrong. Fellowship, worship, teaching, and care for one another are essential. But when these become the primary focus rather than tools for mission, the church loses its way.

Here's a question worth wrestling with: Do you approach your local church asking, "What can I receive?" or "How can I participate in the mission?" Do you evaluate the church based on how well it meets your preferences, or based on how effectively it reaches people who don't yet know Christ?

A fishing boat mentality affects everything. Worship becomes a launching pad for mission rather than just a personal experience. Teaching equips people for ministry rather than just providing information. Fellowship builds relationships that support the mission rather than just social connections.

The beautiful irony? Fishing boat churches often provide deeper satisfaction than cruise ship churches. When people are actively involved in a meaningful mission, they experience the joy that comes from purpose. They develop stronger relationships through shared ministry. They grow spiritually through the challenges of serving others.

Living It Out

Reflection Questions:

1. How would you honestly assess your own mentality—more cruise ship or fishing boat?

2. What would need to change in your church involvement if you fully embraced a fishing boat mentality?

3. How can you help your local church maintain its

mission focus while still caring well for those already in the boat?

Weekly Challenge: This week, approach your church involvement with a fishing boat mentality. Instead of evaluating what you receive, focus on how you can contribute to the mission. Look for one specific way to help "catch fish."

Implementation Ideas:

- Volunteer for an outreach activity or evangelistic event.

- Invite someone to church who doesn't normally attend.

- Offer to help with a ministry that focuses on reaching others.

- Pray specifically for people in your community who don't know Christ.

WEEK 8

FROM FEAR TO FREEDOM

2 Timothy 1:7-8 (AMP) - For God did not give us a spirit of timidity or cowardice or fear, but [He has given us a spirit] of power and of love and of sound judgment and personal discipline [abilities that result in a calm, well-balanced mind and self-control]. So do not be ashamed to testify about our Lord or about me His prisoner...

Corrie ten Boom stood before the concentration camp guard who had been particularly cruel to her sister Betsie. It was after the war, and he was approaching her after a speaking engagement, asking for forgiveness. Every human instinct screamed "fear" and "revenge." But in that moment, Corrie experienced what Paul described to Timothy: "God has not given us a spirit of fear, but of power, love, and sound judgment." Her choice to forgive transformed not only that moment but became a powerful testimony that continues to impact millions worldwide.

Fear is one of the greatest enemies of reliable messengers. It paralyzes our witness, distorts our message, and keeps us anchored when God wants us to take up oars. But Paul reminds Timothy that fear isn't from God—it's a foreign invader in the life of a believer.

The word "fear" here (*deilia*) refers to cowardice or timidity that shrinks back from what should be done. It's different from healthy caution or wise prudence. This is the fear that makes us silent when we should speak, passive when we should act, and withdrawn when we should engage.

Paul contrasts this destructive fear with three powerful gifts God has given us. First, there's **power** (*dunamis*)—the same word used to describe the Holy Spirit's power in Acts 1:8. It's not just human strength or willpower—it's divine enablement that makes us capable of things beyond our natural ability.

Then there's **love** (*agape*). This isn't emotional affection but deliberate commitment to seek others' highest good. Love casts out fear because when we're focused on blessing others, we stop obsessing about protecting ourselves.

Finally, **sound judgment** (*sophronismos*) refers to sensible thinking, self-discipline, and balanced perspective. Fear often distorts our thinking, making small problems seem enormous and temporary setbacks seem permanent. Sound judgment helps us see situations from God's eternal perspective.

Think about the fears that hold messengers back. Fear of rejection: "What if they don't want to hear what I have to say?" Fear of inadequacy: "I don't know enough to represent God well." Fear of failure: "What if I mess up and damage God's reputation?" Fear of persecution: "What if following Christ costs me relationships or opportunities?"

But notice what Paul tells Timothy to do with these fears: "Do not be ashamed of the testimony about our Lord." Instead of hiding from the potential costs of being God's messenger, Timothy should embrace them. Paul himself was in prison when he wrote these words, yet he saw his suffering as part of his calling, not a deviation from it.

The freedom that comes from rejecting fear-based living is extraordinary. When we stop letting fear make our decisions, we discover authentic relationships where we can be genuine instead of performing for approval. We find meaningful purpose, pursuing God's calling instead of playing it safe. We experience spiritual growth through faith risks that develop our character. And we have kingdom impact, participating in God's eternal work instead of just protecting our temporary comfort.

Then there's Jesus, who "for the joy set before Him endured the cross, despising the shame." He didn't minimize the cost of His mission, but He didn't let fear of that cost stop Him from completing it.

Here's what I've discovered: freedom from fear doesn't mean absence of nervous feelings—it means acting in faith despite those feelings. Every reliable messenger in Scripture experienced fear, but they chose to move forward anyway because they trusted in God's power, love, and wisdom. Choosing faith is the difference!

Living It Out

Reflection Questions:

1. What specific fears have been hindering you from fully embracing your role as God's messenger?

2. How have you seen God's power, love, and sound judgment work through you in past situations?

3. What would you attempt for God if you knew you couldn't fail?

Weekly Challenge: Identify one area where fear has been holding you back from being a reliable messenger. Take one concrete step this week to act in faith despite that fear. Remember, courage isn't the absence of fear—it's action in the presence of fear.

Implementation Ideas:

- Memorize 2 Timothy 1:7 and quote it when fear arises.

- Share your fears with a trusted friend who can pray for you and encourage you.

- Study biblical examples of people who overcame fear to serve God faithfully.

- Start a journal documenting how God gives you power, love, and sound judgment in challenging situations.

WEEK 9

THE HOLY SPIRIT: OUR RELIABLE GUIDE

John 16:13-15 (NLT) - When the Spirit of truth comes, he will guide you into all truth. He will not speak on his own but will tell you what he has heard. He will tell you about the future. He will bring me glory by telling you whatever he receives from me.

Hudson Taylor, the famous missionary to China, once wrote, "I have found that there are three stages in every great work of God: first, it is impossible, then it is difficult, then it is done." What made Taylor's impossible work possible wasn't his own strength or wisdom—it was his dependence on the Holy Spirit as his reliable guide. Taylor learned what Jesus promised His disciples: the Spirit of truth would guide them into all truth.

Being a reliable messenger isn't a solo endeavor. Jesus never intended for His followers to represent Him based solely on their own understanding, strength, or wisdom. That's why He promised the Holy Spirit as our Counselor, Advocate, and Guide. The Spirit's role in our lives as messengers is comprehensive and essential.

Jesus describes three crucial ways the Holy Spirit guides reliable messengers. First, **He guides us into all truth**. The phrase "guide into" (*hodegeo*) means to lead along the way, like a skilled guide leading travelers through unfamiliar territory. Truth isn't just information—it's reality as God sees it. The Holy Spirit helps us understand not just what the Bible says, but what it means and how to apply it in specific situations.

Second, **He speaks what He hears**. The Holy Spirit doesn't contradict Scripture or add new revelations beyond what God has already revealed. Instead, He takes the truth of God's Word and makes it come alive in our hearts and minds. He helps us hear God's voice through Scripture, prayer, circumstances, and the counsel of other believers.

Third, **He shows us things to come**. This doesn't necessarily mean predicting the future, but rather helping us understand the eternal significance of present choices and actions. The Spirit gives us perspective that sees beyond immediate circumstances to God's ultimate purposes.

Notice that the Spirit's guidance has a specific focus: glorifying Jesus. "He will bring me glory by telling you whatever he receives from me." This is crucial for reliable messengers to understand. The Holy Spirit's primary work isn't to make us feel good about ourselves or to give us private revelations that elevate us above others. His work is to point us and others to Jesus.

Practical guidance from the Holy Spirit often comes through several channels. There's **Scripture illumination**—as you read God's Word, the Spirit helps specific passages come alive with relevance to your current situation. There's **conviction and comfort**—the Spirit convicts us of sin that hinders our effectiveness as messengers, but He also comforts us with assurance of God's love and forgiveness.

The Spirit provides **gifting and empowerment**, distributing spiritual gifts and providing supernatural ability to serve effectively. He guides through **circumstantial direction**, opening and closing doors of opportunity. And He provides **peace in decision-making**—when facing choices, the Spirit often provides a sense of peace about the right direction.

What I find encouraging is this: dependence on the Holy Spirit transforms how we approach being reliable messengers. Instead of relying solely on our preparation, personality, or persuasive ability, we learn to depend on His power working through us. This doesn't make us passive—it makes us supernaturally effective.

Think about the disciples before and after Pentecost. Before receiving the Holy Spirit, they were fearful, confused, and ineffective. After Pentecost, these same men turned the world upside down with their message. The difference wasn't better training or favorable circumstances—it was the Holy Spirit's power working through surrendered lives.

Living It Out

Reflection Questions:

1. How have you experienced the Holy Spirit's guidance in your life as God's messenger?

2. What prevents you from depending more fully on the Spirit's leadership rather than your own understanding?

3. In what current situation do you need the Spirit's guidance to be a more reliable messenger?

Weekly Challenge: Before each significant conversation or interaction this week, pause and ask the Holy Spirit to guide your words and actions. Pay attention to how He leads you to respond differently than you might have naturally.

Implementation Ideas:

- Develop a habit of praying for the Spirit's guidance before important conversations.

- Study biblical examples of people who were led by the Spirit.

- Practice listening-prayer—spending time in silence to hear from God.

- Look for ways the Spirit might be speaking through Scripture, circumstances, and other believers.

WEEK 10

FAITHFUL WITNESSES IN JERUSALEM

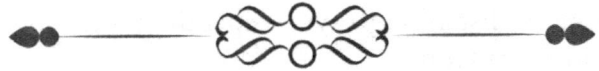

Acts 1:8 (ESV) - "But you will receive power when the Holy Spirit has come upon you, and you will be my witnesses in Jerusalem and in all Judea and Samaria, and to the end of the earth."

William Carey, known as the father of modern missions, is famous for his work in India. But before he ever left England, Carey spent years faithfully witnessing in his own village as a shoemaker and lay preacher. His heart for distant lands was cultivated through faithful service in his own "Jerusalem." He understood Jesus' strategy: reliable messengers start where they are before they go somewhere else.

Jesus' final instructions to His disciples provide the geographic and strategic blueprint for reliable messengers: "You will be my witnesses in Jerusalem and in all Judea and Samaria, and to the end of the earth." This wasn't a multiple-choice option where disciples could pick their preferred location. It was a progressive sequence that begins at home.

Interestingly enough, Jerusalem actually represents the place where you are right now—your family, workplace, neighborhood, and immediate sphere of influence. It's the place where people know you best, where your character is most visible, and where your witness carries both the greatest potential impact and the greatest personal cost.

Why does Jesus start with Jerusalem? Several important reasons emerge here. First, **authenticity is tested at home**. It's easier to impress strangers than to influence family members who know your flaws. If your faith can't make a difference in your closest relationships, its power to transform distant ones is questionable.

Second, **character is built through proximity**. Those closest to us see us in our worst moments as well as our best. Learning to represent Christ well when we're tired, stressed, or frustrated builds the character necessary for more public ministry.

Then there's this: **love proves itself locally**. Jesus said people would know His disciples by their love for one another. This love is first demonstrated in how we treat those closest to us—spouses, children, parents, siblings, and close friends.

Finally, **foundation precedes expansion**. Just like a building needs a solid foundation before it can rise tall, our witness needs to be established locally before it can expand globally. Skipping Jerusalem often leads to ministry that looks impressive from a distance but lacks depth and authenticity.

The disciples' experience illustrates this principle. After Pentecost, they began witnessing in Jerusalem—the very city where Jesus had been crucified, where the religious leaders opposed them, and where their own failures were well known. Yet this was where their witness began to transform lives.

Think about the characteristics of faithful Jerusalem witnesses. They start with relationships, not programs. They combine words with works. They persist despite rejection. And they see ordinary moments as opportunities.

Your Jerusalem might be challenging. Perhaps your family thinks your faith is too intense. Maybe your coworkers are skeptical about Christianity. Your neighbors might seem uninterested in spiritual conversations. But this is exactly where Jesus wants you to begin.

Remember this: you don't have to be perfect to be a faithful witness in your Jerusalem. The disciples had failed Jesus during His crucifixion, yet He still commissioned them to be His witnesses. Your past mistakes don't disqualify you—they can become part of your testimony about God's grace.

Living It Out

Reflection Questions:

1. Who are the people in your immediate "Jerusalem" who need to see Christ through your life?

2. What opportunities for being a witness do you encounter regularly that you might be overlooking?

3. How might God want to use your current relationships and circumstances to advance His kingdom?

Weekly Challenge: Focus intentionally on being a faithful witness in your Jerusalem this week. Choose three people in your immediate sphere of influence and pray specifically for opportunities to represent Christ well to them through both words and actions.

Implementation Ideas:

- Map out your personal "Jerusalem"—identify your key relationships and spheres of influence.

- Look for natural opportunities to serve or encourage those closest to you.

- Practice sharing your faith story in simple, natural ways.

- Ask God to show you how your daily activities can become opportunities for witness.

WEEK 11

THE MESSAGE WE CARRY

1 Corinthians 15:1-4 (ESV) - Now I would remind you, brothers, of the gospel I preached to you... For I delivered to you as of first importance what I also received: that Christ died for our sins in accordance with the Scriptures, that he was buried, that he was raised on the third day...

(Story Inspired by True Events) During World War II, radio operators carried life-and-death messages across dangerous territory. The success of military operations often depended on these messengers transmitting their communications accurately and completely. They couldn't edit the message to make it more appealing or easier to deliver. They couldn't add personal opinions or leave out parts they didn't like. The message had to be delivered exactly as received, because lives depended on its accuracy.

Paul understood this principle when he reminded the Corinthians of the gospel message he had delivered to them. He uses specific language: "For I delivered to you as of first importance what I also received." Paul saw himself as a link in a chain of reliable messengers, faithfully passing on the essential message exactly as he had received it.

The gospel that Paul describes contains four essential elements that every reliable messenger must understand and communicate. First: **"Christ died for our sins in accordance with the Scriptures."** This addresses the problem of human sin and God's solution. It's not just that Christ died—many people have died. It's that He died specifically "for our sins," taking the penalty we deserved.

Second: "**He was buried.**" This confirms the reality of Christ's death. He wasn't merely unconscious or in a temporary state—He was literally dead and placed in a tomb. The burial validates the completeness of His sacrifice and the reality of what followed.

Third: "**He was raised on the third day in accordance with the Scriptures.**" This is the heart of the Christian message. The resurrection isn't just about life after death—it's about victory over death itself. Christ didn't just survive death; He conquered it.

Fourth: "**He was seen.**" The resurrection wasn't a private mystical experience but a public, verifiable event. Paul lists multiple witnesses, including himself. This message isn't based on philosophical speculation but on historical testimony from reliable witnesses.

Notice what Paul doesn't include in this essential gospel message. He doesn't mention specific methods of evangelism, particular worship styles, denominational distinctives, or cultural preferences. The gospel is remarkably simple and remarkably universal.

But here's what excites me: simplicity doesn't mean the message lacks power. Paul reminds the Corinthians that this gospel "is the power of God to salvation for everyone who believes." The message itself carries supernatural power to transform lives when faithfully delivered.

This creates both confidence and responsibility for reliable messengers. We can be confident because we're not depending on our own persuasive ability—we're delivering a message that

God has promised to honor. We carry responsibility because we must deliver the message accurately and completely.

Consider how this applies to your role as a reliable messenger. Clarity over cleverness—your goal isn't to impress people with theological sophistication but to clearly communicate the simple truth. Completeness over comfort—all four elements are necessary. Faithfulness over innovation—while we should communicate in ways people understand, we can't change the essential content. Dependence over self-reliance—the power is in the message, not in the messenger.

The gospel message that each of us carry is the same message that transformed the apostles, changed the early church, and has been rescuing people for two thousand years. It's the message that transformed your own life. You don't need to improve it, just deliver it faithfully.

Living It Out

Reflection Questions:

1. How would you explain the essential gospel message to someone who had never heard it?

2. Which part of the gospel message do you find most challenging to communicate clearly?

3. How does knowing you carry God's powerful message change your confidence as His messenger?

Weekly Challenge: Practice articulating the gospel message clearly and simply. Find opportunities this week to share the essential elements of Christ's death, burial, and resurrection with someone who needs to hear it.

Implementation Ideas:

- Write out your personal explanation of the gospel in simple, clear language.

- Memorize key verses that communicate the gospel message effectively.

- Practice sharing the gospel in natural conversation rather than formal presentations.

- Study how different biblical characters communicated the gospel message to various audiences.

WEEK 12

DEO-CENTRIC LIVING

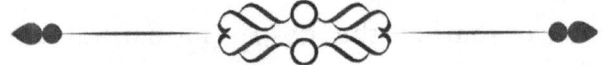

Colossians 3:16-17 (AMP) - Let the [spoken] word of Christ have its home within you [dwelling in your heart and mind— permeating every aspect of your being]... Whatever you do [no matter what it is] in word or deed, do everything in the name of the Lord Jesus...

Brother Lawrence was a 17th-century monk who worked in the monastery kitchen. While others sought God through elaborate spiritual disciplines, Lawrence discovered something profound: he could live in constant communion with God while washing dishes, preparing meals, and completing mundane tasks. His secret was learning to do everything "in the name of the Lord Jesus." His simple approach to deo-centric living—God-centered living— transformed not only his own spiritual experience but influenced countless others through his letters, later compiled in "The Practice of the Presence of God."

Paul's instruction in Colossians reveals the heart of deo-centric living: "Let the word of Christ dwell in you richly... And whatever you do in word or deed, do all in the name of the Lord Jesus." This isn't about adding religious activities to secular life—it's about transforming all of life into worship and witness.

Deo-centric living begins with internal transformation. "Let the word of Christ dwell in you richly." The word "dwell" (*katoikeo*) means to settle down permanently, like making a house your home. Christ's word isn't just visiting your mind occasionally—it's taking up permanent residence, influencing every thought, decision, and response.

When Scripture becomes our mental furniture, something remarkable happens. Instead of reacting to situations based on emotions, cultural norms, or personal preferences, we begin responding from biblical truth. This creates a completely different way of being in the world.

Deo-centric living naturally flows into relationships. Paul mentions teaching and admonishing one another with psalms, hymns, and spiritual songs. When God is truly the center of our lives, we can't help but influence others toward Him.

But here's the revolutionary part: deo-centric living transforms ordinary activities. "Whatever you do in word or deed, do all in the name of the Lord Jesus." There's no distinction between sacred and secular activities when everything is done for God's glory and in Jesus' name.

Consider what this means practically. Your work becomes ministry when you perform it with excellence as service to Christ. Your parenting becomes discipleship when you see it as stewarding souls God has entrusted to you. Your friendships become evangelism when you represent Christ's love in them. Your recreation becomes worship when you enjoy God's gifts with gratitude. Your challenges become character development when you face them trusting God's sovereignty.

The phrase "in the name of the Lord Jesus" doesn't mean adding "in Jesus' name" to the end of prayers. It means acting as Jesus' representative, with His authority, for His purposes, and in His character. When you do something "in someone's name," you're acting on their behalf and according to their will.

This creates natural accountability. Before speaking, acting, or responding, deo-centric living asks: "Can I do this as Jesus' representative? Does this align with His character and purposes? Will this bring glory to God?"

Deo-centric living culminates in gratitude: "Giving thanks to God the Father through Him." When God is truly the center of our lives, gratitude becomes our default response. We recognize that everything good comes from Him, every opportunity is His gift, and every ability we have is His provision.

The opposite of deo-centric living is ego-centric living— making ourselves the center of everything. I've seen the difference this makes. Ego-centric living asks, "What's in this for me?" Deo-centric living asks, "How does this serve God's purposes?"

Living It Out

Reflection Questions:

1. In what areas of your life is God truly the center, and in what areas are you still the center?

2. How would your daily activities change if you consistently did them "in the name of the Lord Jesus"?

3. What would others notice about your life if you lived with consistent gratitude to God?

Weekly Challenge: Choose three regular activities this week (work tasks, household chores, interactions with family) and intentionally do them "in the name of the Lord Jesus." Notice how this changes your attitude and approach.

Implementation Ideas:

- Before starting each day, surrender your plans and activities to God's purposes.

- Practice breath prayers throughout the day to maintain God-awareness.

- Look for ways to serve others in every environment you enter.

- End each day by thanking God for specific ways He worked through your activities.

WEEK 13

QUARTER 1
REVIEW/INTEGRATION

2 Timothy 3:16-17 (AMP) - All Scripture is God-breathed [given by divine inspiration] and is profitable for instruction, for conviction [of sin], for correction [of error and restoration to obedience], for training in righteousness...

George Müller, the great man of faith who cared for thousands of orphans in 19th-century England, made a remarkable discovery early in his Christian life. Instead of beginning his days with newspapers or personal concerns, he started each morning by reading Scripture until his soul was "happy in the Lord." This simple practice of making God's Word central to his daily experience became the foundation for a life of extraordinary faith and service. Müller understood what Paul taught Timothy: Scripture is the reliable foundation for every reliable messenger.

As we conclude this first quarter of our journey, let's consider what we've discovered about becoming reliable messengers. We've learned that reliability isn't about perfection—it's about faithfulness, integrity, and competence developed through relationship with God. We've heard God's call to carry His message and discovered He equips those He calls. We've experienced the refreshing power that comes through faithful service.

We've made crucial paradigm shifts—from parishioner to

practitioner, from anchors to oars, from cruise ship to fishing boat mentality, from fear to freedom. Each shift has prepared us for more effective service as God's messengers.

We've discovered the Holy Spirit as our reliable guide, learned to be faithful witnesses in our own Jerusalem, and understood the essential message we carry. And we've explored what it means to live a deo-centric life where everything we do is done in the name of the Lord Jesus.

Paul's description of Scripture's nature and purpose provides the essential framework for all we've learned. When Paul says "All Scripture is given by inspiration of God," he's making a foundational claim about the Bible's unique authority and reliability. The word "inspiration" (*theopneustos*) literally means "God-breathed." Just as God breathed into Adam the breath of life, God breathed into Scripture, making it a living Word.

This God-breathed nature makes Scripture uniquely profitable for four essential functions. There's **teaching**—providing the content of our faith. There's **reproof**—exposing error and convicting of sin. There's **correction**—showing us how to make things right. And there's **instruction in righteousness**—training us like a coach trains an athlete.

The ultimate purpose? "That the man of God may be complete, thoroughly equipped for every good work." Scripture doesn't just provide theoretical knowledge—it prepares us for effective service.

Notice the progression: Scripture teaches us what to believe, reproves us when we're wrong, corrects our errors, and trains us in righteousness, so that we become complete and equipped for good works. This is exactly what reliable messengers need—not just biblical knowledge, but biblical character and competence.

As we move forward into the next quarter, where we'll study biblical examples of reliable messengers, remember that these foundations are essential. Every effective messenger in Scripture built on these same foundations—they were called by God, equipped by His Spirit, transformed by His Word, and committed to His purposes.

The enemy understands the power of a biblio-centric life, which is why he consistently attacks the authority, relevance, and clarity of Scripture. If he can get us to doubt God's Word, add to it, subtract from it, or ignore it, he has effectively neutralized us as reliable messengers.

But here's what I want you to remember: when God's Word truly becomes central to your life—not just something you read but something that reads you, not just information you gather but transformation you experience—you become the kind of reliable messenger who brings healing to a world stumbling in trouble.

Living It Out

Reflection Questions:

1. Looking back over these thirteen weeks, what has been the most significant change in your understanding of being a reliable messenger?

2. Which paradigm shift (parishioner to practitioner, anchors to oars, cruise ship to fishing boat, fear to freedom) has been most challenging for you?

3. How has your relationship with God's Word changed through this first quarter of study?

Weekly Challenge: Take time this week to review your notes and reflections from the past thirteen weeks. Identify three specific commitments you want to make as you continue your journey toward becoming a more reliable messenger.

Implementation Ideas:

- Create a personal mission statement based on what you've learned about being a reliable messenger.

- Share with someone else the most important insight you've gained from this first quarter.

- Develop a plan for maintaining the spiritual disciplines that will sustain you as a reliable messenger.

- Prepare your heart for the next quarter by asking God to teach you through the biblical examples you'll study.

QUARTER 2
BIBLICAL EXAMPLES OF RELIABLE MESSENGERS

Learning from Scripture's Messengers (Weeks 14-26)

Old Testament Examples (Weeks 14-22)

WEEK 14

ELIJAH: STANDING ALONE FOR TRUTH

1 Kings 18:20-24 (ESV) - So Ahab sent to all the people of Israel and gathered the prophets together at Mount Carmel. And Elijah came near to all the people and said, "How long will you go limping between two different opinions? If the Lord is God, follow him; but if Baal, then follow him."

In 1955, a soft-spoken seamstress named Rosa Parks boarded a Montgomery city bus after a long day of work. When the driver ordered her to give up her seat to a white passenger, Parks quietly refused. She later said, "I was not tired physically... No, the only tired I was, was tired of giving in." Her solitary act of courage—one woman standing alone against an unjust system—sparked the Montgomery Bus Boycott and became a catalyst for the entire Civil Rights Movement. Parks understood something profound: sometimes one person willing to stand alone for truth can change the world. She wasn't seeking fame or recognition; she was simply unwilling to compromise what she knew was right, regardless of the personal cost.

On a mountainside in Israel, one man faced 450 prophets of Baal and 400 prophets of Asherah. The odds were overwhelming—850 to 1 to be exact. The political pressure was enormous as Queen Jezebel had made serving the true God a capital offense. The cultural momentum was against him because the majority of Israel had embraced pagan worship. But Elijah understood something that made him fearless: reliable messengers don't derive their confidence from public opinion polls. They derive it from the God who sends them.

The confrontation on Mount Carmel represents one of history's greatest examples of a reliable messenger standing alone for truth. But here's what's remarkable—Elijah's reliability wasn't demonstrated just in this dramatic moment. It was built through years of faithful obedience in smaller tests.

Reliable messengers speak truth regardless of consequences. When Elijah first appeared to King Ahab, he delivered a message of the coming drought. Not exactly what any king wanted to hear. Elijah could have softened the message, found a more diplomatic way to say it, or waited for a more convenient time. Instead, he delivered God's word exactly as he received it.

During the drought, God provided for Elijah uniquely through the ravens, then through a poor widow. Elijah learned to depend completely on God's supernatural provision rather than human systems of support. This freed him to speak boldly without fear of losing financial backing or political favor.

On Mount Carmel, Elijah forced Israel to choose: "How long will you falter between two opinions? If the Lord is God, follow Him; but if Baal, follow him." He refused to let people remain comfortable in spiritual compromise. Sometimes being a reliable messenger means forcing decisions that people would prefer to avoid.

But Elijah didn't just argue theology with the false prophets—he proposed a test that would reveal whose God was real. He understood that reliable messengers must be willing to put God's reputation on the line, trusting Him to vindicate His own truth.

The details of Elijah's challenge reveal his complete confidence in God. He not only proposed the test but made it more difficult for himself by soaking his sacrifice with water three times. He wasn't trying to hedge his bets—he was demonstrating absolute trust in God's power.

When the fire fell and consumed not just the sacrifice but the stones, dust, and water, the people's response was immediate: "The Lord, He is God! The Lord, He is God!" Truth demonstrated with power is irresistible.

But notice what happened next. Elijah, fresh from this incredible victory, ran from Queen Jezebel's threats and hid in a cave, feeling isolated and defeated. Even reliable messengers experience human emotions and spiritual lows. What matters isn't the absence of struggle but the willingness to continue serving despite it.

God's gentle restoration of Elijah reveals important truths. God provides rest for weary servants—before addressing Elijah's emotional state, God let him sleep and provided food. God speaks in whispers, not just windstorms—the "still small voice" reminded Elijah that God's power doesn't always manifest dramatically. God has others who remain faithful— Elijah thought he was alone, but God had 7,000 others who hadn't bowed to Baal.

Standing alone for truth doesn't mean you're actually alone. It means you're willing to be the only visible representative of God's truth in your circumstances, trusting that God sees, God knows, and God will vindicate His word in His timing.

Living It Out

Reflection Questions:

1. Where in your life do you feel pressure to compromise God's truth for social acceptance or personal advantage?

2. How has God provided for you in past situations when standing for truth was costly?

3. What "Mount Carmel moment" might God be preparing you for where His truth needs to be demonstrated through your life?

Weekly Challenge: Identify one situation this week where you need to stand for God's truth even if it means standing alone. Ask God for Elijah's courage to represent Him faithfully regardless of opposition.

Implementation Ideas:

- Study other biblical examples of people who stood alone for truth.

- Develop convictions about which biblical principles are non-negotiable in your life.

- Find encouragement from other believers who will support you in taking difficult stands.

- Remember that God's approval matters more than human approval.

WEEK 15

ABRAHAM: THE FRIEND OF GOD

Genesis 12:1-3 (ESV) - Now the Lord said to Abram, "Go from your country and your kindred and your father's house to the land that I will show you. And I will make of you a great nation, and I will bless you and make your name great, so that you will be a blessing."

(Story Inspired by True Events) In 1519, Spanish conquistador Hernán Cortés made one of history's most audacious decisions. After landing on the shores of Mexico with just 600 men to face the mighty Aztec Empire, Cortés ordered his men to burn their ships. His soldiers were stunned—without ships, there was no retreat, no backup plan, no safety net. When asked why he would make such a drastic choice, Cortés replied, "If we are going forward, we cannot be looking back." While Cortés' motives were questionable, his principle was sound: extraordinary achievements often require burning the bridges to ordinary life.

At age 75, when most people are settling into retirement, Abraham received a call that would change not only his life but the entire course of human history. God's instruction was clear but challenging: "Go from your country and your kindred and your father's house to the land that I will show you." Abraham's response established him as one of history's most reliable messengers—not because he never faltered, but because he consistently chose faith over fear, obedience over comfort, and God's promises over present circumstances.

What made Abraham such a reliable messenger? His story reveals several key characteristics. First, reliable messengers respond to God's call with radical obedience. Abraham's obedience wasn't partial or delayed. Genesis 12:4 simply states, "So Abram departed as the Lord had spoken to him." He didn't negotiate terms, demand guarantees, or wait for more convenient timing. When God spoke, Abraham moved.

This kind of radical obedience seems almost reckless to our modern sensibilities. We want detailed plans, guaranteed outcomes, and clear explanations before we commit to major changes. But Abraham demonstrates that reliable messengers often must move forward with incomplete information, trusting God's character more than their circumstances.

Notice also that reliable messengers become sources of blessing to others. God's promise to Abraham was personal— "I will make of you a great nation... I will bless you and make your name great"—but it had a global purpose: "you shall be a blessing... and in you all the families of the earth shall be blessed."

Here's a crucial truth: God blesses us not just for our own sake but so we can be conduits of blessing to others. Abraham's wealth, influence, and spiritual legacy were meant to benefit not just his descendants but all nations. Every reliable messenger must grapple with this tension between receiving God's blessings and sharing them with others.

For 25 years, Abraham waited for the promised son. During this time, he and Sarah aged well beyond natural child-bearing years. The circumstances seemed to contradict God's promise daily. Yet Romans 4:20-21 tells us that Abraham "did not waver at the promise of God through unbelief, but was strengthened in faith, giving glory to God, and being fully convinced that what He had promised He was also able to perform."

This doesn't mean Abraham never struggled with doubt. Genesis records moments when he tried to help God fulfill His promises through human effort (like having a son with Hagar). But his overall trajectory was faithfulness to God's word despite overwhelming evidence to the contrary.

Abraham didn't just personally follow God—he led his entire household to do the same. Genesis 18:19 reveals God's confidence in Abraham: "I have known him, in order that he may command his children and his household after him, that they keep the way of the Lord, to do righteousness and justice."

Many people compartmentalize their faith, being one person in public and another at home. Abraham demonstrates that reliable messengers must be consistent witnesses in their most intimate relationships. The people who know us best should be the ones most impressed by our faithfulness to God.

Abraham's willingness to offer Isaac as a sacrifice represents the ultimate test of reliability. God asked him to surrender not just his son but the very means through which God's promises would be fulfilled. Abraham's obedience revealed that he valued his relationship with God more than even his most precious earthly relationships.

James 2:23 tells us that Abraham "was called the friend of God." This friendship wasn't based on casual acquaintance but on proven reliability over decades of testing. God could trust Abraham with difficult assignments because Abraham had demonstrated consistent faithfulness.

The same opportunity exists for us. God is still looking for friends He can trust with His purposes, people who will say yes to His call regardless of the cost or the mystery involved.

Living It Out

Reflection Questions:

1. What has God called you to do that requires stepping out of your comfort zone in faith?

2. How are you being a source of blessing to others through the gifts and opportunities God has given you?

3. In what areas of your life do you need to trust God's promises despite contradictory circumstances?

Weekly Challenge: Take one step of faith this week that demonstrates your trust in God's promises. Whether it's starting a difficult conversation, making a sacrificial gift, or beginning a new ministry, let your actions show that you believe God's word.

Implementation Ideas:

- Study God's promises in Scripture and identify which ones you need to trust more fully.

- Look for ways to bless others through the resources God has entrusted to you.

- Practice immediate obedience in small things to build your capacity for larger acts of faith.

- Consider what relationships or priorities might need to be surrendered to follow God's call more fully.

WEEK 16

MOSES: THE RELUCTANT BUT FAITHFUL MESSENGER

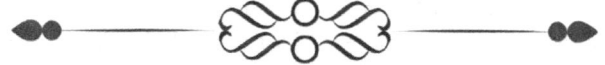

Exodus 4:10-16 (ESV) - But Moses said to the Lord, "Oh, my Lord, I am not eloquent, either in the past or since you have spoken to your servant, but I am slow of speech and of tongue." Then the Lord said to him, "Who has made man's mouth? Who makes him mute, or deaf, or seeing, or blind? Is it not I, the Lord?"

In 1940, King George VI of England faced an impossible situation. His country was at war, his people needed encouragement, and as their monarch, he was expected to deliver inspiring speeches to rally the nation. There was just one problem: the king had a severe speech impediment that made public speaking agonizing. Every logical reason suggested he should let someone else be the voice of Britain during its darkest hour. Instead, with the help of a speech therapist and tremendous personal courage, King George VI became one of the most inspiring voices of World War II. His Christmas broadcast in 1939 included the famous lines: "I said to the man who stood at the gate of the year, 'Give me a light that I may tread safely into the unknown.' And he replied, 'Go out into the darkness and put your hand into the hand of God.'"

Standing before a burning bush that wasn't consumed, Moses focused on his inadequacies rather than God's power. His reluctance makes his eventual faithfulness all the more remarkable and encouraging for every believer who has ever felt unqualified for God's calling.

Moses' initial resistance reveals several misconceptions that often hinder potential messengers. There's the myth of natural qualification—Moses assumed that being God's messenger required natural eloquence, charisma, and communication skills. But God's response was revealing: "Who has made man's mouth? Is it not I, the Lord?" God wasn't looking for naturally talented speakers; He was looking for available servants.

This is encouraging for everyone who feels inadequate for God's calling. Your weaknesses don't disqualify you—they become opportunities for God to display His strength through you. As Paul later wrote, "God has chosen the foolish things of the world to put to shame the wise, and God has chosen the weak things of the world to put to shame the things which are mighty."

Moses' concern about his speaking ability revealed a deeper fear: What if I fail? What if I embarrass myself and God? What if the people don't listen? These fears are natural but not decisive. God's calling isn't based on our ability to guarantee success—it's based on His ability to work through willing servants.

Notice how God addressed Moses' fear. He didn't minimize the challenge or promise it would be easy. Instead, He promised His presence: "I will be with your mouth and teach you what you shall say." God's presence is always sufficient for God's assignments.

When God persisted in calling Moses, his final objection was essentially, "Send someone else!" This reveals the human tendency to assume others are better qualified for significant service. While humility is admirable, false humility that refuses

God's call is actually disobedience.

Despite his initial reluctance, Moses became one of history's most reliable messengers. What transformed him? As Moses obeyed step by step, he experienced God's power working through him. The plagues in Egypt, the Red Sea crossing, and the provision in the wilderness built his confidence—not in himself, but in God.

Moses learned to see beyond his own inadequacies to the needs of the people he was called to serve. The Israelites' slavery mattered more than his speech impediment. The mission was bigger than his fears.

Exodus 33:11 tells us something remarkable: "The Lord spoke to Moses face to face, as a man speaks to his friend." Moses' intimacy with God grew through years of faithful service. This relationship became the foundation of his effectiveness as a messenger.

Moses developed a heart for the people he served. When they sinned and faced God's judgment, Moses interceded for them, even offering to have his own name blotted out if it would save them. Reliable messengers care more about others' welfare than their own reputation.

Here's what Moses teaches us: God's calling doesn't depend on natural ability. Your weaknesses don't limit God's power—they provide opportunities for His strength to be displayed. Obedience is more important than eloquence. Experience builds confidence as you step out in faith.

Moses reminds us that God specializes in using unlikely messengers. If you feel unqualified for what God is calling you to do, you're in good company. The question isn't whether you feel adequate—it's whether you're willing to let God work through your availability.

Living It Out

Reflection Questions:

1. What aspects of God's calling in your life make you feel inadequate or reluctant?

2. How have you seen God work through your weaknesses in past situations?

3. What would you attempt for God if you knew He would provide everything necessary for success?

Weekly Challenge: Take one step this week toward something God has been calling you to do despite your feelings of inadequacy. Trust that His presence will be sufficient for whatever He's asking of you.

Implementation Ideas:

- List your perceived inadequacies and ask God how He might use them for His glory.

- Study other biblical examples of unlikely messengers (Gideon, David, Esther, Mary).

- Find a mentor who can encourage you in areas where you feel weak.

- Start with small acts of obedience to build confidence for larger challenges.

WEEK 17

SAMUEL: HEARING GOD'S VOICE

1 Samuel 3:1-10 (ESV) - Now the boy Samuel was ministering to the Lord in the presence of Eli. And the word of the Lord was rare in those days... Then the Lord called Samuel, and he said, "Here I am!"... Therefore Eli said to Samuel, "Go, lie down, and if he calls you, you shall say, 'Speak, Lord, for your servant hears.'"

In 1876, Alexander Graham Bell was working late in his Boston laboratory, trying to perfect his revolutionary invention—the telephone. His assistant, Thomas Watson, was in another room with the receiving device when Bell accidentally spilled acid on his clothes. Without thinking, he called out, "Mr. Watson, come here! I want to see you!" To Bell's amazement, Watson came running, excited and breathless. "I heard you!" Watson exclaimed. "I heard every word you said distinctly!" That first transmitted human voice changed everything. But here's what's remarkable: Watson almost didn't recognize that the strange sounds coming from the device were actually Bell's voice. He had to learn to distinguish between random noise and meaningful communication.

In the darkness of the tabernacle, a young boy heard his name called three times. Each time he ran to Eli, thinking the old priest had summoned him. It took three attempts before Eli realized what was happening: God was speaking to Samuel. The priest's instruction was simple but profound: "Go, lie down; and it shall be, if He calls you, that you must say, 'Speak, Lord, for Your servant hears.'"

Samuel's story provides us crucial principles about how reliable messengers develop the ability to hear from God. First, learning to distinguish God's voice requires practice. Samuel didn't immediately recognize God's voice. The text tells us "Samuel did not yet know the Lord, nor was the word of the Lord yet revealed to him." Hearing God's voice is both a learned skill that develops through experience and a dependence on the Holy Spirit at work in your life.

This is encouraging for believers who struggle with discerning God's direction. Like Samuel, we can learn to recognize God's voice through practice, patience, and the guidance of mature believers who help us understand when God is speaking.

Samuel was sleeping in the tabernacle, near the ark of God. He had positioned himself in God's presence. While God can speak anywhere at any time, He often speaks to those who deliberately seek Him in prayer, Scripture study, and worship. The phrase "The lamp of God had not yet gone out" suggests this happened just before dawn—those quiet moments when distractions are minimal and our hearts are receptive.

Eli taught Samuel to say, "Speak, Lord, for Your servant hears." Notice the order—"Speak, Lord" comes before "Your servant hears." Samuel was learning to give God permission to speak whatever He wanted, not just what Samuel wanted to hear. The word "servant" indicates Samuel's recognition that hearing from God creates responsibility.

Now here's the challenging part: God's first message to Samuel was difficult. It was a judgment against Eli's house because of his sons' wickedness and Eli's failure to restrain them. This wasn't an encouraging prophecy or a comfortable truth—it was a hard word that would be painful to deliver.

After Samuel faithfully delivered this first difficult word, "the Lord was with him and let none of his words fall to the ground." God honored Samuel's faithfulness by continuing to speak through him. Eventually, "all Israel from Dan to Beersheba knew that Samuel had been established as a prophet of the Lord."

Samuel's lifelong ministry demonstrates several characteristics of reliable messengers who hear from God. There's consistency—Samuel continued to hear from God throughout his life. There's courage—he delivered unpopular messages to kings and people alike. There's integrity—when he challenged Israel to point out any way he had failed them, they couldn't identify a single instance. And there's intercession— Samuel continued to pray for Israel even when they rejected his counsel.

Learning to hear God's voice is essential for every reliable messenger. While not everyone is called to be a prophet like Samuel, every believer needs to discern God's direction for their life and ministry.

Living It Out

Reflection Questions:

1. How do you currently position yourself to hear from God in prayer, Scripture, and worship?

2. What helps you distinguish between God's voice and your own thoughts or desires?

3. When has God spoken to you about something difficult that required courage to obey or share?

Weekly Challenge: Practice positioning yourself to hear from God this week. Set aside specific times for listening-prayer, and when you sense God speaking, respond with Samuel's heart: "Speak, Lord, for Your servant hears."

Implementation Ideas:

- Develop a consistent time and place for listening-prayer.

- Study how God's voice is described throughout Scripture.

- Find mature believers who can help you discern when God is speaking.

- Keep a journal of times when you sense God's direction and how those situations develop.

WEEK 18

NATHAN: SPEAKING TRUTH TO POWER

2 Samuel 12:1-7 (ESV) - And the Lord sent Nathan to David. He came to him and said to him, "There were two men in a certain city, the one rich and the other poor..."

In 1963, a young Baptist preacher stood on the steps of the Lincoln Memorial facing a crowd of 250,000 people and the most powerful political leaders in America. But Martin Luther King Jr.'s most courageous moments didn't come when he delivered his famous "I Have a Dream" speech to supporters who agreed with him. They came in private meetings with President Kennedy and other officials who preferred the status quo. Like the Old Testament prophet Nathan confronting King David, King had to find ways to help powerful people see uncomfortable truths about themselves and their policies.

The prophet Nathan stood before King David, the most powerful man in Israel, with a message that could cost him his life. David had committed adultery with Bathsheba and arranged for her husband Uriah to be killed in battle. Everyone in the palace knew what had happened, but no one dared confront the king. Everyone except Nathan.

Nathan's confrontation of David represents one of the clearest examples in Scripture of a reliable messenger speaking truth to power. His approach provides a masterclass in how to deliver difficult truth with both courage and wisdom.

First, reliable messengers prioritize God's authority over human authority. Nathan understood that ultimate authority belongs to God, not to earthly rulers. While he showed appropriate respect for David's position as king, he didn't let that respect prevent him from delivering God's message of judgment.

This principle applies to every believer in positions where they must choose between pleasing people and pleasing God. Whether it's confronting a supervisor about unethical practices, challenging a friend about destructive behavior, or speaking truth in family relationships where others prefer comfortable lies, reliable messengers understand that God's approval matters more than human approval.

Notice Nathan's wisdom in his approach. He didn't burst into the throne room shouting accusations. He told a story that engaged David's sense of justice and allowed the king to condemn the behavior before realizing it was his own. The story bypassed David's defensive mechanisms, engaged his conscience, demonstrated that David still had moral sensibility, and made David's own words the basis for judgment.

Nathan's approach shows that speaking truth doesn't require being harsh or insensitive. Reliable messengers can be both truthful and tactful, both courageous and wise.

After David's confession, Nathan could have stopped with a comforting word about forgiveness. Instead, he delivered God's complete message, including the consequences David would face: "The sword shall never depart from your house... I will raise up adversity against you from your own house."

Here's what I've observed: reliable messengers don't edit God's message to make it more palatable. They understand that people need to hear both the severity of sin and the reality of consequences, not just the comfort of forgiveness.

Nathan's confrontation led to David's repentance and restoration. The goal wasn't to destroy David but to bring him back into right relationship with God. Psalm 51, David's psalm of repentance, shows the depth of restoration that followed Nathan's faithful confrontation.

When reliable messengers speak truth to power, their motivation should always be restoration, not revenge or personal vindication. They confront because they care, not because they want to prove they're right.

Nathan didn't disappear after delivering his difficult message. He continued to serve as David's counselor and later played a key role in ensuring Solomon's succession to the throne. This shows that speaking truth, when done with the right motives and proper approach, can actually strengthen relationships rather than destroy them.

Speaking truth to power is never easy, but it's often necessary. Consider the various "powers" in your own life—employers, family members, friends, community leaders—who might need to hear difficult truths from someone who cares about them.

The principles from Nathan's example apply whether you're confronting a small issue or a major crisis. Pray for wisdom about timing and approach. Check your motives—are you speaking truth because you care about the person and want restoration? Use appropriate channels—make sure you have the right standing to address the issues you see. And prepare for various responses—not everyone will respond positively to the truth.

Nathan reminds us that reliable messengers sometimes must risk relationships and personal safety to deliver God's truth. But when done with wisdom, courage, and love, such confrontations can lead to genuine repentance and restored relationships.

Living It Out

Reflection Questions:

1. Who in your life might need to hear a difficult truth that others are afraid to speak?

2. How can you develop the wisdom to speak truth in ways that lead to restoration rather than defensiveness?

3. What fears keep you from confronting issues that you know need to be addressed?

Weekly Challenge: Ask God to show you if there's a "David" in your life who needs to hear a difficult truth. If He reveals someone, pray about the right approach and timing, then have the courage to speak with love and wisdom.

Implementation Ideas:

- Study Jesus' methods of confronting sin and error in the Gospels.

- Practice having difficult conversations about smaller issues to build your skills.

- Develop relationships that give you credibility to speak into people's lives.

- Remember that the goal is always restoration and growth, not winning arguments.

WEEK 19

ISAIAH: THE WILLING VOLUNTEER

Isaiah 6:1-8 (ESV) - In the year that King Uzziah died I saw the Lord sitting upon a throne, high and lifted up... And I said: "Woe is me! For I am lost; for I am a man of unclean lips..."

(Story with Representative Reflection) On September 12, 2001, the day after the devastating terrorist attacks on America, President George W. Bush stood in the Oval Office facing the greatest crisis of his presidency. Intelligence reports suggested more attacks were likely, the nation was in chaos, and world leaders were calling for immediate military response. In that moment of overwhelming responsibility, Bush later recalled thinking, "I never asked for this. I never wanted to be a wartime president." But then he remembered something his father had taught him: "When history calls, you don't get to choose the timing or the circumstances—you only get to choose your response."

The temple was filled with smoke, and the foundations shook at the voice of the seraphim crying, "Holy, holy, holy is the Lord of hosts; the whole earth is full of His glory!" In this overwhelming vision of God's holiness, Isaiah experienced a sequence that would transform him from a religious observer into a reliable messenger: he saw God's glory, recognized his own sinfulness, received God's cleansing, heard God's call, and volunteered for service.

Unlike Moses' reluctance or Jonah's resistance, Isaiah's response was immediate and enthusiastic: "Here am I! Send me."

Isaiah's calling experience reveals the essential elements that create willing, reliable messengers. First, a vision of God's holiness produces proper perspective. Isaiah's encounter began with seeing "the Lord sitting on a throne, high and lifted up." This vision of God's exalted position put everything else in proper perspective. Kings and kingdoms that seemed so important from an earthly viewpoint were revealed as temporary and subordinate to God's eternal throne.

Reliable messengers need this perspective. When we truly grasp God's sovereignty, holiness, and eternal purposes, our earthly concerns—reputation, comfort, security—take their proper place. We're able to take risks for God because we see Him as infinitely greater than any earthly power or problem.

Isaiah's response to God's holiness wasn't pride in his religious position but deep conviction: "Woe is me! For I am lost; for I am a man of unclean lips, and I dwell in the midst of a people of unclean lips; for my eyes have seen the King, the Lord of hosts!"

This conviction was necessary preparation for service. Isaiah couldn't be a reliable messenger while harboring unconfessed sin or self-righteousness. The seraph's act of touching Isaiah's lips with a coal from the altar symbolized the cleansing that makes reliable service possible.

After his sin was purged, Isaiah was ready to represent God. He understood that his ability to serve didn't come from his natural qualifications but from God's cleansing and calling. This gave him confidence to volunteer for whatever assignment God had in mind.

Now notice something crucial: Isaiah volunteered before he knew what the job would entail. God hadn't yet explained the difficulty of the mission—that people would hear but not understand, see but not perceive. This willingness to serve without knowing all the details is characteristic of reliable messengers. They trust God's character more than they fear unknown challenges.

When God finally revealed Isaiah's mission, it was sobering. He would preach to people who would largely reject his message. Yet Isaiah faithfully served for over 40 years, delivering God's messages of both judgment and hope to a largely unresponsive people.

Isaiah's ministry demonstrates that reliable messengers must be motivated by obedience to God rather than positive response from people. Some messengers serve in contexts where they see dramatic results; others serve where results are minimal. Both are equally valuable if they're faithful to their calling.

Isaiah's prophetic ministry produced some of the most beautiful and powerful passages in Scripture, including detailed prophecies about the coming Messiah. His willingness to serve in difficult circumstances contributed to God's eternal purposes in ways he probably never fully understood during his lifetime.

The pattern of Isaiah's calling—vision, conviction, cleansing, commission, volunteering—remains relevant for everyone God calls to be His messenger. Seek vision of God's greatness through worship and Scripture. Welcome conviction that leads to cleansing and growth. Receive God's cleansing through confession and repentance. Listen for God's call and volunteer willingly—say "Here am I, send me" before you know all the details.

Living It Out

Reflection Questions:

1. When have you had a vision or experience of God's holiness that changed your perspective on everything else?

2. What areas of your life might need God's cleansing before you can serve Him more effectively?

3. How would your service change if you focused more on faithfulness to God than on positive responses from people?

Weekly Challenge: Practice Isaiah's response this week: "Here am I, send me." Look for opportunities to volunteer for service before you know all the details, trusting God's character more than your own understanding.

Implementation Ideas:

- Spend time in worship focusing specifically on God's holiness and sovereignty.

- Ask God to reveal any areas of your life that need cleansing for more effective service.

- Look for service opportunities where you can volunteer without knowing all the outcomes.

- Study Isaiah's prophecies to see how his difficult ministry contributed to God's eternal purposes.

WEEK 20

JEREMIAH: THE PERSISTENT PROPHET

Jeremiah 1:4-10 (NLT) - The Lord gave me this message: "I knew you before I formed you in your mother's womb. Before you were born I set you apart and appointed you as my prophet to the nations."

In 1940, Winston Churchill stood alone among world leaders, warning that Nazi Germany posed an existential threat to civilization. For years, politicians had dismissed him as a warmonger and extremist. The British public wanted to hear about peace, not preparation for war. Churchill's warnings about Hitler's intentions were so unpopular that he was excluded from government positions and ridiculed in the press. But Churchill refused to soften his message or abandon his post as a watchman. Month after month, year after year, he delivered the same unwelcome warning: "The storm is coming. We must prepare."

"I knew you before I formed you in your mother's womb. Before you were born I set you apart and appointed you as my prophet to the nations." With these words, God commissioned a young man who would become known as the "weeping prophet"—not because he was weak, but because he felt deeply the pain of delivering difficult messages to people he loved.

Jeremiah's 40-year ministry would be marked by rejection, persecution, and apparent failure, yet his persistence in delivering God's word makes him one of history's most reliable messengers.

Jeremiah's calling and ministry reveal essential truths about persistence in difficult assignments. First, God's calling is often contrary to human preferences. Jeremiah's immediate response to God's call was resistance: "O Sovereign Lord, I can't speak for you! I'm too young!" Like Moses, Jeremiah focused on his perceived inadequacies rather than God's enablement.

God's response was direct: "Don't say, 'I'm too young,' for you must go wherever I send you and say whatever I tell you." God wasn't asking for Jeremiah's opinion about his suitability—He was announcing His decision and promising His support.

God told Jeremiah his ministry would involve both destruction and construction: "Today I appoint you to stand up against nations and kingdoms. Some you must uproot and tear down, destroy and overthrow. Others you must build up and plant." Sometimes we must confront sin, challenge complacency, and disturb comfortable deceptions before we can build healthy spiritual foundations.

Jeremiah faced constant opposition throughout his ministry. The people rejected his messages, religious leaders persecuted him, and political authorities imprisoned him. At one point, he was thrown into a cistern and left to die. Yet God had warned him from the beginning: "They will fight against you, but they shall not prevail against you, for I am with you to deliver you."

Here's what Jeremiah learned: opposition to God's message doesn't mean the messenger is wrong—it often means the message is accurate and needed. Reliable messengers must expect resistance and prepare to persist despite it.

What I find remarkable about Jeremiah is his emotional transparency. He complained to God about his circumstances, questioned the justice of his treatment, and sometimes wished he had never been born. Yet he continued delivering God's messages despite his emotional struggles.

This teaches us that reliable messengers don't have to be emotionally perfect—they have to be faithful. God can use people who struggle with discouragement, loneliness, and frustration as long as they continue obeying His call.

Anyone can deliver a popular message or serve when conditions are favorable. But Jeremiah continued preaching for 40 years to people who largely rejected his message. He watched the nation ignore his warnings and suffer the consequences he had predicted. Yet he remained faithful to his calling.

This kind of persistence reveals the difference between reliable messengers and merely talented communicators. Reliable messengers are motivated by obedience to God, not by positive response from people.

From a human perspective, Jeremiah's ministry was unsuccessful. The people didn't repent, the nation went into exile, and Jerusalem was destroyed. But God's purposes were accomplished through Jeremiah's faithful preaching. His prophecies prepared a remnant for restoration, provided hope during exile, and contributed to Scripture that continues to guide believers today.

Jeremiah's ministry offers encouragement to every believer called to persist in difficult circumstances. Difficult assignments often indicate God's confidence in you. Emotional struggles are compatible with faithful service. Success is measured by faithfulness, not results. And persistence reveals character—

continuing to serve when it's hard reveals the depth of your commitment to God.

Living It Out

Reflection Questions:

1. What difficult assignment has God given you that requires persistence despite opposition or discouragement?

2. How do you handle emotional struggles while maintaining faithfulness to God's calling?

3. Where do you need to measure success by faithfulness rather than visible results?

Weekly Challenge: Identify one area where you've been tempted to give up or compromise because of resistance or lack of visible results. Commit to persisting in faithfulness for another week, trusting God's purposes more than human responses.

Implementation Ideas:

- Study Jeremiah's prayers and complaints to learn how to be emotionally honest with God while remaining obedient.

- Find encouragement from other believers who have persisted through difficult assignments.

- Remember that God's timeline often differs from human expectations.

- Focus on faithfulness to God's call rather than positive response from people.

WEEK 21

EZEKIEL: THE WATCHMAN ON THE WALL

Ezekiel 3:16-21 (ESV) - "Son of man, I have made you a watchman for the house of Israel. Whenever you hear a word from my mouth, you shall give them warning from me."

(Story Inspired by True Events) During the London Blitz of World War II, thousands of civilians volunteered to serve as air raid wardens and fire watchers. They climbed to the highest points in the city—church steeples, apartment rooftops, and observation towers—scanning the skies for incoming German bombers. When they spotted enemy aircraft, these watchers had one job: sound the alarm as loudly and quickly as possible. Their success wasn't measured by how many people heeded the warning or found shelter—it was measured by whether they faithfully sounded the alert.

In ancient cities, watchmen stood on the walls scanning the horizon for approaching danger. Their job wasn't to fight the enemy—it was to sound the alarm when trouble was coming. God appointed Ezekiel to serve as a spiritual watchman, responsible for warning people about spiritual danger whether they wanted to hear it or not.

Ezekiel's role as a watchman reveals a crucial aspect of being a reliable messenger: the responsibility to warn others about spiritual danger, regardless of how they respond to the warning.

God told Ezekiel, "If I say to the wicked, 'You shall surely die,' and you give him no warning... that wicked person shall die for his iniquity, but his blood I will require at your hand."

This establishes a sobering principle: reliable messengers are accountable to God for delivering warnings, not for ensuring people respond positively to them. Ezekiel couldn't control whether people listened to his warnings, but he was responsible for giving them.

"Yet, if you warn the wicked, and he does not turn from his wickedness, nor from his wicked way, he shall die in his iniquity; but you have delivered your soul." This distinction is crucial for reliable messengers. We're responsible for giving warnings when God directs us to do so. We're not responsible for making people accept those warnings. Our accountability to God is based on our faithfulness to speak, not on others' willingness to listen.

But here's something important: God's instruction to Ezekiel included warning righteous people who turned away from their righteousness. This teaches us that being a reliable messenger sometimes means confronting believers who are compromising their faith, not just reaching unbelievers with the gospel.

God instructed Ezekiel to use vivid object lessons, symbolic actions, and graphic illustrations to communicate His messages. Ezekiel lay on his side for 390 days, ate bread cooked over dung, and performed other unusual acts that made people uncomfortable but got their attention.

Sometimes reliable messengers must use unconventional methods to break through people's spiritual complacency. While we should always be wise and appropriate, we shouldn't let social comfort prevent us from delivering necessary warnings.

While much of Ezekiel's ministry involved warnings about coming judgment, he also delivered messages of hope and restoration. Chapters like Ezekiel 36 and 37 (the valley of dry bones) promised that God would eventually restore His people.

Reliable messengers understand that warnings about spiritual danger must be balanced with hope about spiritual rescue. We warn people about the consequences of sin not to condemn them but to motivate them to seek God's salvation and restoration.

Ezekiel's calling cost him his reputation (people thought he was strange), his comfort (he had to perform difficult symbolic acts), and even his wife (God told him not to mourn her death publicly as an object lesson about coming judgment).

Being a reliable messenger often requires personal sacrifice. People may misunderstand your motives, question your methods, or reject your warnings. But the watchman's responsibility to warn others takes priority over personal comfort and social acceptance.

The principle of watchman ministry applies to every believer in various contexts. Parents serve as watchmen for their children. Friends serve as watchmen for each other. Church members serve as watchmen for their congregations. Citizens serve as watchmen for their communities. Employees serve as watchmen in their workplaces.

The key principles for effective watchman ministry? Stay alert to spiritual dangers others might miss. Speak courageously even when warnings are unwelcome. Trust God with results— your job is to sound the alarm, not force people to respond. Balance warning with hope. And accept the cost—being a watchman often involves personal sacrifice and social rejection.

Living It Out

Reflection Questions:

1. In what relationships or contexts might God be calling you to serve as a spiritual watchman?

2. What spiritual dangers do you see around you that need to be addressed, even if doing so is uncomfortable?

3. How do you balance giving necessary warnings with maintaining loving relationships?

Weekly Challenge: Ask God to make you alert to spiritual dangers in your sphere of influence. If He shows you someone who needs a warning about spiritual risk, have the courage to speak with love and wisdom.

Implementation Ideas:

- Develop spiritual discernment through regular prayer and Scripture study.

- Practice giving gentle warnings in smaller situations to build courage for larger ones.

- Study how Jesus warned people about spiritual dangers while still showing love.

- Find support from other believers who understand the responsibility of watchman ministry.

WEEK 22

DANIEL: STANDING FIRM IN BABYLON

Daniel 1:8-16 (ESV) - But Daniel resolved that he would not defile himself with the king's food, or with the wine that he drank. Therefore he asked the chief of the eunuchs to allow him not to defile himself.

(Story with Representative Quote) In 1961, a young Air Force captain named Chuck Yeager was selected to be part of America's first astronaut program. But there was a problem: Yeager refused to compromise his principles to advance his career. While other test pilots were willing to play political games and tell officials what they wanted to hear, Yeager insisted on giving honest assessments about aircraft safety, even when those assessments delayed projects and angered superiors. Years later, Yeager reflected, "I could have been an astronaut if I'd been willing to bend a little, to go along to get along. But I learned early that your integrity is like your shadow—it follows you everywhere, and once you lose it, it's almost impossible to get back."

Fifteen-year-old Daniel stood in the palace of the most powerful empire in the world, faced with a choice that would define the rest of his life. King Nebuchadnezzar had ordered that he and his Jewish friends be fed from the royal table—an honor most captives would eagerly accept. But Daniel "resolved that he would not defile himself with the king's food, or with the wine that he drank."

Daniel's story provides a masterclass in how to be a faithful messenger of God while living and working in environments that oppose your values.

First, reliable messengers make non-negotiable commitments before facing pressure. Daniel's decision wasn't made in the moment of testing—it was a predetermined commitment. The phrase "resolved" (or "purposed in his heart") indicates a settled resolution made before the crisis. This advance commitment gave him strength to resist when pressure came.

This principle applies to every believer living in secular environments. We need to decide in advance which biblical principles are non-negotiable, so we're not caught off guard when pressure comes to compromise.

Daniel's refusal to eat the king's food might seem like a minor issue, but it established his character and demonstrated his reliability. This small act of faithfulness led to greater opportunities to serve and influence the empire. God honored Daniel's faithfulness by making him healthier and wiser than those who ate the royal food.

Daniel didn't withdraw from Babylonian society or refuse to serve in the government. Instead, he served with such excellence that he was promoted to positions of great authority. Yet he never compromised his faith or adopted pagan practices.

This balance—engagement without compromise—is essential for believers in secular environments. We're called to be salt and light in the world, which requires both involvement and distinctiveness.

Throughout his career, Daniel served four different kings: Nebuchadnezzar, Belshazzar, Darius, and Cyrus. In each case, his faithfulness created opportunities to speak God's truth to the most powerful people in the known world. His reliability as a messenger gave him access to influence that most people never experience.

Despite his excellent service and proven loyalty, Daniel faced persecution. Jealous officials tricked King Darius into signing a law that made prayer to anyone except the king illegal for 30 days. They knew Daniel would continue praying to God regardless of the consequences.

Daniel's response reveals the heart of a reliable messenger: "When Daniel knew that the writing was signed, he went home. And in his upper room, with his windows open toward Jerusalem, he knelt down on his knees three times that day, and prayed and gave thanks before his God, as was his custom since early days."

Daniel didn't make a public show of his civil disobedience, but he didn't hide it either. He continued his normal pattern of prayer, trusting God with the consequences.

The famous result was protection in the lions' den. God shut the lions' mouths, and Daniel emerged unharmed. King Darius was so impressed that he issued a decree acknowledging the power of Daniel's God.

While God doesn't always provide miraculous protection, He does honor faithfulness. Sometimes that protection is miraculous; sometimes it comes through natural means; sometimes it includes suffering that ultimately accomplishes God's purposes.

Daniel's influence extended far beyond his lifetime. His

prophecies provided hope for God's people during exile and pointed toward the coming Messiah. His example of faithfulness in hostile environments continues to encourage believers today.

Daniel's principles for serving as a reliable messenger in hostile environments include making non-negotiable commitments in advance, serving with excellence, maintaining spiritual disciplines, looking for opportunities to influence leaders, accepting the cost of faithfulness, and trusting God's protection and timing.

Living It Out

Reflection Questions:

1. What non-negotiable commitments do you need to make about maintaining your faith in your current environment?

2. How can you serve with greater excellence in your secular responsibilities while maintaining your spiritual distinctiveness?

3. What opportunities might God be giving you to influence people in positions of authority or responsibility?

Weekly Challenge: Identify one area where you've been tempted to compromise your faith for social acceptance or professional advancement. Make a Daniel-like commitment to maintain your integrity in that area, trusting God with the results.

Implementation Ideas:

- Write down your non-negotiable biblical commitments

and review them regularly.

- Look for ways to serve with excellence in your secular responsibilities.

- Maintain consistent spiritual disciplines regardless of your environment.

- Pray for opportunities to influence those in authority over you or around you.

New Testament Examples (Weeks 23-26)

WEEK 23

JOHN THE BAPTIST: PREPARING THE WAY

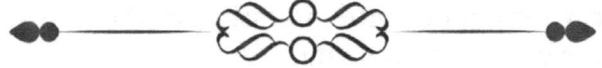

Matthew 3:1-6 (ESV) - In those days John the Baptist came preaching in the wilderness of Judea, "Repent, for the kingdom of heaven is at hand."

In 1904, a young engineer named John Frank Stevens was hired to oversee the construction of the Panama Canal, one of the most ambitious engineering projects in history. When Stevens arrived in Panama, he found chaos: workers were dying from disease, equipment was rusting in the jungle, and previous efforts had failed spectacularly. Stevens realized that before any canal could be built, he needed to prepare the way—establish hospitals, build railroads, create sanitation systems, and organize supply chains. For two years, Stevens focused not on digging the canal but on preparing the infrastructure that would make the canal possible. His critics called him overly cautious, but Stevens understood a fundamental truth: preparation work is often invisible but always essential.

In the wilderness of Judea, a wild-looking man dressed in camel's hair stood in the Jordan River baptizing crowds of people while proclaiming, "Repent, for the kingdom of heaven is at hand!" John the Baptist understood his role perfectly: he was the opening act for the greatest messenger in history. Jesus Himself said, "Among those born of women there has not risen one greater than John the Baptist."

John's ministry reveals essential characteristics of reliable messengers who understand their role in God's larger purposes. First, reliable messengers focus on their mission, not their comfort. John could have ministered in Jerusalem's temple, wearing fine clothes and enjoying a prestigious religious position. Instead, he chose the wilderness, wore rough clothing, ate locusts and wild honey, and preached to whoever would come hear him.

The message takes priority over the messenger. John's preaching was direct and uncompromising: "Repent!" He didn't soften the message to make it more appealing. His goal was to prepare hearts to receive the Messiah, which required honest confrontation with sin.

When religious leaders came to be baptized, John called them a "brood of vipers" and challenged them to "bear fruits worthy of repentance." This wasn't harsh for the sake of being harsh—it was a necessary truth that cut through religious pretense to reach the heart.

But here's what I love about John: when Jesus appeared, John's disciples were concerned that people were leaving to follow Him instead. John's response revealed the heart of a true messenger: "He must increase, but I must decrease."

John understood that his role was temporary and preparatory. His success was measured not by how many followers he gained but by how effectively he prepared people to recognize and follow Jesus.

John didn't limit his message to safe religious topics. When King Herod married his brother's wife, John publicly declared, "It is not lawful for you to have her." This confrontation eventually cost John his life, but he understood that reliable messengers must speak truth regardless of the personal consequences.

John's preaching created such spiritual hunger that "Jerusalem, all Judea, and all the region around the Jordan went out to him and were baptized by him in the Jordan, confessing their sins." People were ready to receive Jesus when He arrived because John had prepared their hearts.

This is a crucial function of reliable messengers—creating spiritual hunger in others. Sometimes we prepare people to receive ministry from someone else rather than being the primary instrument of their transformation.

When John was in prison, he sent disciples to ask Jesus, "Are You the Coming One, or do we look for another?" This question came from the same man who had proclaimed Jesus as "the Lamb of God who takes away the sin of the world!"

John's doubt doesn't diminish his reliability as a messenger. Instead, it shows his humanity. Reliable messengers can struggle with questions while remaining faithful to their calling.

John's ministry was relatively brief—about three and a half years. Yet his impact was profound. He prepared the way for Jesus, baptized the Messiah, and influenced disciples who later became apostles. His example of faithful service in a supporting role continues to inspire believers today.

John the Baptist reminds us that some of the most important ministry happens behind the scenes, preparing others to receive what God wants to give them. Reliable messengers understand that their greatest success may be measured by someone else's effectiveness.

Living It Out

Reflection Questions:

1. How is God calling you to prepare others to receive His truth or follow His calling?

2. In what ways do you need to decrease so that Christ can increase in your relationships and ministry?

3. What truths do you need to speak even if they might be costly or unpopular?

Weekly Challenge: Look for one opportunity this week to prepare someone else for spiritual growth or ministry effectiveness. Focus on their development rather than your own recognition.

Implementation Ideas:

- Identify people you can mentor or prepare for greater spiritual responsibility.

- Practice pointing people to Jesus rather than seeking credit for spiritual conversations.

- Look for ways to create spiritual hunger in others through your example and words.

- Accept that your most important ministry may be preparing others to succeed.

WEEK 24

THE TWELVE: FROM FOLLOWERS TO LEADERS

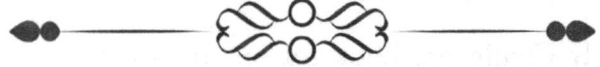

Mark 3:13-19 (ESV) - And he went up on the mountain and called to him those whom he desired, and they came to him. And he appointed twelve (whom he also named apostles) so that they might be with him and he might send them out to preach...

(Story Inspired by True Events) In 1943, a gruff Marine drill instructor named Sergeant Major John Basilone was assigned an impossible task: transform a group of untested recruits into Marines capable of fighting in the Pacific Theater. The young men who reported to Parris Island came from all walks of life—farm boys from Iowa, factory workers from Detroit, college students from California. They had little in common except their willingness to serve. Years later, one of his former recruits wrote: "Sergeant Basilone didn't just teach us how to be Marines—he showed us. By the time we shipped out, we weren't just following orders—we were following a leader we trusted completely."

They were an unlikely group: fishermen, a tax collector, a political revolutionary, and various other ordinary men with no formal religious training. Yet Jesus "appointed twelve, that they might be with Him and that He might send them out to preach." Over the course of three years, these common men were transformed from followers into leaders, from students into teachers, from observers into participants.

The selection and development of the twelve disciples reveals Jesus' strategy for creating reliable messengers. First, Jesus chose ordinary people with extraordinary potential. The disciples weren't religious scholars, wealthy businessmen, or political leaders. They were working-class men with various backgrounds and personalities. Peter was impulsive, Thomas was skeptical, Matthew had a questionable past, and Simon was politically radical.

This selection demonstrates that God often chooses people based on their availability and teachability rather than their natural qualifications. The disciples' transformation shows what's possible when ordinary people commit to following Jesus wholeheartedly.

Notice this: Jesus appointed the twelve "that they might be with Him and that He might send them out to preach." The order matters—being with Jesus came before being sent by Jesus. Relationships were the foundation for the mission.

This principle is crucial for developing reliable messengers. Before people can effectively represent Christ to others, they must spend time with Christ themselves. Ministry flows out of intimacy, not just training or technique.

The Gospels show Jesus teaching the disciples through multiple methods: direct instruction, parables and stories, modeling, hands-on experience, and correction and feedback. This multi-faceted approach recognizes that people learn differently and need various types of input to develop fully as reliable messengers.

When Jesus sent the twelve out to minister, they returned excited about their success: "Lord, even the demons are subject to us in Your name!" But they also experienced failures, like their inability to cast out a demon that required prayer and fasting.

Both experiences were educational. Success built their confidence in God's power working through them; failure taught them their dependence on God and the need for spiritual preparation.

Jesus was patient with their slow development. The disciples regularly misunderstood Jesus' teaching, competed for positions of prominence, and showed surprising spiritual density. Yet Jesus continued investing in them, knowing that transformation takes time.

This patience is essential for anyone involved in developing reliable messengers. People don't change overnight, and spiritual growth often involves setbacks as well as progress.

Compare the disciples before and after Pentecost. Before, they argued about who was greatest; after, they served one another humbly. Before, they fled when Jesus was arrested; after, they boldly preached despite persecution. Before, they had trouble understanding Jesus' teaching; after, they articulated the gospel clearly to diverse audiences.

This transformation didn't happen because of better training or more favorable circumstances—it happened because of the Holy Spirit's power working through their continued relationship with the risen Christ.

Each disciple developed unique strengths while sharing core commitments. Peter became the bold spokesman, John became known for love, Matthew wrote a Gospel for Jewish audiences, and Thomas eventually became a missionary to distant lands. They maintained their individual personalities while developing shared characteristics as reliable messengers.

The twelve didn't just become effective messengers themselves—they developed others who developed others. The early church grew explosively because these men understood that their job was to reproduce reliable messengers, not just be them.

The principles from Jesus' development of the twelve apply to everyone involved in spiritual formation. Start with relationships before trying to teach or correct. Use multiple learning approaches. Expect gradual development. Be patient with questions and mistakes. Focus on character as well as competence. Encourage individual strengths within shared commitments. And emphasize reproduction—the goal isn't just mature believers but mature believers who can develop others.

Living It Out

Reflection Questions:

1. Who has invested in your development as a reliable messenger the way Jesus invested in the twelve?

2. What combination of learning approaches (teaching, modeling, experience, correction) do you need most right now?

3. How are you investing in developing others to become reliable messengers?

Weekly Challenge: Identify someone you can begin investing in the way Jesus invested in the disciples. Start by building relationships and looking for opportunities to model faithful living.

Implementation Ideas:

- Study Jesus' methods of developing the disciples throughout the Gospels.

- Look for natural mentoring opportunities in your current relationships.

- Practice using multiple approaches to help others grow spiritually.

- Be patient with gradual development in yourself and others.

WEEK 25

PAUL: FROM PERSECUTOR TO PROCLAIMER

Acts 9:1-22 (ESV) - But Saul, still breathing threats and murder against the disciples of the Lord, went to the high priest... Now as he went on his way, he approached Damascus, and suddenly a light from heaven shone around him.

Klaus Fuchs was a brilliant young physicist who fled Nazi Germany and eventually joined the top-secret Manhattan Project to develop the atomic bomb. For years, Fuchs was considered one of the most trusted scientists on the project. But unknown to his colleagues, Fuchs was secretly passing atomic secrets to the Soviet Union. When his espionage was discovered in 1950, the scientific community was stunned. Yet what happened next was even more remarkable: after serving his prison sentence, Fuchs completely abandoned his communist sympathies and spent the rest of his life advocating for nuclear disarmament. His former colleagues struggled to understand how someone could switch sides so completely—not once, but twice.

The most feared enemy of the early church was traveling to Damascus with letters authorizing him to arrest any Christians he found there. Saul of Tarsus was "breathing threats and murder against the disciples of the Lord," determined to eliminate what he saw as a dangerous heresy. Then a blinding light from heaven stopped him in his tracks, and a voice asked,

"Saul, Saul, why are you persecuting Me?"

Within days, the church's greatest persecutor became its most passionate proclaimer. Paul's transformation remains one of history's most dramatic examples of how God can turn the most unlikely person into a reliable messenger.

Paul's conversion and subsequent ministry reveal profound truths about God's ability to transform lives. First, God can transform anyone, regardless of their past. Saul's credentials as an enemy of Christianity were impeccable. He was present at Stephen's stoning, "ravaged the church," and was authorized by religious authorities to arrest believers wherever he found them.

Yet God saw beyond Saul's actions to his heart. The same passion that made him a fierce persecutor would make him an incredible messenger when redirected toward God's purposes. God specializes in redemptive transformation that turns weaknesses into strengths and enemies into ambassadors.

Within days of his encounter with Christ, Saul was preaching in the synagogues "that He is the Son of God." His transformation was so complete and immediate that "all who heard were amazed, and said, 'Is this not he who destroyed those who called on this name in Jerusalem?'"

While not every conversion is as dramatic as Paul's, genuine transformation always produces observable change. Reliable messengers have experienced real change in their own lives, which gives authenticity to their message about God's transforming power.

Paul's background as a Pharisee gave him deep knowledge of Scripture and Jewish culture. His Roman citizenship provided legal protection and cultural access. His training in Greek philosophy helped him communicate with Gentile audiences. God didn't waste Paul's pre-conversion experiences—He redeemed them for kingdom purposes.

This principle encourages everyone who wonders if their background disqualifies them from serving God effectively. God can use your education, work experience, cultural background, and even your past mistakes as preparation for future ministry.

After his conversion, Paul spent three years in Arabia and then returned to Damascus. When he tried to join the disciples in Jerusalem, they were afraid of him. He had to be vouched for by Barnabas before they would accept him.

Paul's early years included rejection by both Christians (who didn't trust him) and Jews (who saw him as a traitor). This period of difficulty was essential preparation for his later ministry. God often uses challenging seasons to develop the character necessary for effective service.

Paul's ministry was characterized by boldness, adaptability, endurance, humility, and reproduction. He preached fearlessly despite constant opposition. He became "all things to all men" to win some. He continued ministering for approximately 30 years despite beatings, shipwrecks, and imprisonment. He called himself "the least of the apostles" and "the chief of sinners." And he didn't just plant churches—he developed leaders like Timothy, Titus, and many others.

Paul's transformation encourages everyone who feels disqualified by their past. If God could transform a persecutor into an apostle, He can transform anyone into a reliable messenger. Past failures, mistakes, or even rebellion don't disqualify you from future service. Instead, they can become part of your testimony about God's transforming grace.

The principles from Paul's conversion and ministry? No one

is beyond God's reach. Authentic transformation produces authentic witness. God redeems all experiences for His purposes. Expect opposition and preparation periods. And focus on reproduction—develop other reliable messengers who can continue the work.

Living It Out

Reflection Questions:

1. What aspects of your background or past experiences might God want to redeem for His purposes?

2. How has your personal transformation given you credibility to speak about God's power to change lives?

3. Who in your sphere of influence seems unlikely to become a believer but might be someone God is preparing to transform?

Weekly Challenge: Share your transformation story with someone this week—how God has changed you and what difference it has made in your life. Use Paul's example to encourage someone who feels disqualified by their past.

Implementation Ideas:

- Write out your personal testimony focusing on God's transforming power.

- Look for ways your unique background equips you for specific ministry opportunities.

- Be patient with people who seem hostile to the gospel— God may be preparing their hearts.

- Focus on developing others who can continue spreading the message of transformation.

WEEK 26

TIMOTHY: THE FAITHFUL APPRENTICE

2 Timothy 1:3-7 (AMP) - I thank God, whom I worship and serve with a clear conscience the way my forefathers did, as I constantly remember you in my prayers night and day... I remember your sincere and unqualified faith...

In 1503, a thirteen-year-old boy named Raffaello Sanzio knocked on the door of Pietro Perugino's workshop in Perugia, Italy. The boy had shown artistic promise, but he was just another aspiring painter in a city full of them. Perugino could have dismissed the young apprentice or assigned him to menial tasks. Instead, he saw something special—a teachable spirit, careful attention to detail, and genuine humility. For the next four years, Perugino invested deeply in his young apprentice. The world came to know him as Raphael, one of history's greatest artists. But Raphael never forgot his master's investment, later saying, "I learned from Perugino not just how to hold a brush, but how to see beauty, how to persist through failure, and how to pour my soul into my work."

In a culture that celebrated self-made success, Timothy represented something very different: the power of faithful apprenticeship. Raised by a godly grandmother and mother, mentored by the apostle Paul, and developed through years of faithful service, Timothy became one of the early church's most reliable messengers not through natural charisma or dramatic conversion, but through consistent faithfulness and teachable humility.

Timothy's development reveals essential principles about how reliable messengers are formed. First, spiritual heritage provides foundation. Timothy's faith was rooted in the "genuine faith that is in you, which dwelt first in your grandmother Lois and your mother Eunice." He didn't start from spiritual ground zero—he built on a foundation laid by faithful women who invested in his spiritual development.

Remember that Paul became Timothy's spiritual father, taking him on missionary journeys, teaching him through both instruction and experience, and eventually entrusting him with significant responsibilities. This mentoring relationship was mutually beneficial—Paul gained a faithful companion and eventual successor, while Timothy gained invaluable training and opportunity.

The mentor-apprentice relationship remains one of the most effective ways to develop reliable messengers. Formal education has its place, but nothing replaces learning from someone who models faithful service in real-world situations.

Paul's letters to Timothy focus as much on character issues as on ministry techniques. He emphasizes Timothy's need to "kindle afresh the gift of God," to "not be ashamed," and to "be strong in the grace that is in Christ Jesus."

This balanced approach recognizes that reliable messengers need both competence and character. Skills without character lead to ministry failure; character without skills limits ministry effectiveness.

Paul had to encourage Timothy not to let others despise his youth and to overcome his natural timidity. Even well-prepared messengers face obstacles that require encouragement and support.

Here's what Timothy's struggles remind us: being a reliable messenger doesn't mean being naturally fearless or confident. It means being faithful despite fears and limitations.

Paul didn't give Timothy major responsibilities right away. He started as a traveling companion, then took on specific assignments in established churches, then finally was entrusted with oversight of the pivotal church in Ephesus.

This progression shows wisdom in developing reliable messengers. Too much responsibility too soon can overwhelm developing leaders; too little responsibility for too long can frustrate those ready for greater challenges.

By the end of Paul's life, Timothy had become so reliable that Paul could write, "For I have no one else [like him who is] so kindred a spirit who will be genuinely concerned for your [spiritual] welfare."

The apprenticeship was successful not because Timothy became identical to Paul, but because he became a reliable messenger in his own right, carrying forward the essential commitments while expressing them through his own personality and gifts.

Timothy's example provides a model for both mentors and apprentices. For mentors: look for people with teachable hearts, invest deeply in a few, balance instruction with experience, focus on character development, gradually increase responsibilities, and develop people to surpass your own effectiveness.

For apprentices: seek out mentors who model what you want to become, be teachable and responsive to feedback, prove faithful in small responsibilities, focus on character development, remember that development takes time, and plan to mentor others as you grow.

Timothy's story encourages both those who feel unprepared for ministry and those who feel ready to serve but lack opportunity. Whether you need mentoring or are ready to mentor others, Timothy's example shows that reliable messengers are developed through faithful relationships over time.

Living It Out

Reflection Questions:

1. Who has served as a "Paul" in your life, and how have they helped develop you as a reliable messenger?

2. What characteristics of a good apprentice do you need to develop further?

3. Who might God be calling you to mentor as your "Timothy"?

Weekly Challenge: If you need mentoring, take a step this week to connect with someone who could help develop your effectiveness as God's messenger. If you're ready to mentor, look for someone you could begin investing in consistently.

Implementation Ideas:

- Identify the character qualities you most need to develop and find ways to work on them.

- Look for experienced believers who model effective ministry and ask for their guidance.

- If you're mentoring others, focus on their character

development as much as their ministry skills.

- Remember that both mentoring and being mentored are long-term commitments that require patience.

QUARTER 3
THE MAKING OF RELIABLE MESSENGERS

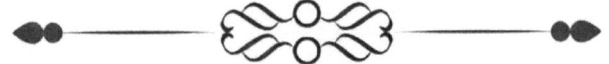

Development and Discipleship (Weeks 27-39)

The Equipping Process

WEEK 27

THE EQUIPPING PROCESS

Ephesians 4:11-16 (NLT) - Now these are the gifts Christ gave to the church: the apostles, the prophets, the evangelists, and the pastors and teachers. Their responsibility is to equip God's people to do his work and build up the church, the body of Christ.

In 1935, automotive pioneer Henry Ford was facing a crisis. His assembly line workers could build cars efficiently, but when something broke down, production stopped until specialized mechanics could fix the problem. Meanwhile, his competitor General Motors was training every worker to understand multiple aspects of car manufacturing. Ford realized he needed to change his approach. Instead of having workers who could only perform one task, he needed to equip every employee with broader skills and knowledge. Ford instituted comprehensive training programs where experienced supervisors taught not just what to do, but why they were doing it and how their role connected to the bigger picture. Within two years, Ford's factories were running more smoothly than ever. Ford later reflected, "I thought my job was to hire hands, but I discovered I needed to develop minds."

Paul's description of the church in Ephesians 4 reveals that God has provided everything needed to develop reliable messengers—spiritual gifts, leadership roles, clear purposes, and the Holy Spirit's power. But like those products requiring assembly, these elements must be properly connected and activated to achieve God's intended results.

Paul's explanation of the equipping process reveals God's comprehensive strategy for developing reliable messengers. First, God gives gifts to the church for developing people: "And He Himself gave some to be apostles, some prophets, some evangelists, and some pastors and teachers." These leadership gifts aren't ends in themselves—they're God's tools for developing the whole body of Christ.

The five-fold ministry gifts each contribute something essential to the equipping process. **Apostles** provide pioneering vision and church-planting leadership. **Prophets** deliver God's timely messages and call people to righteousness. **Evangelists** focus on reaching the lost and training others in evangelism. **Pastors** provide care, protection, and spiritual nurturing. **Teachers** explain Scripture and help people understand and apply God's truth.

But here's the crucial insight: "for the equipping of the saints for the work of ministry." The phrase reveals God's strategy. Leaders aren't meant to do all the ministry while everyone else watches—they're meant to equip others to do ministry.

This represents a fundamental shift from consumer Christianity to contributor Christianity. Instead of hiring professionals to perform spiritual services, the church is designed to develop every member into an active participant in God's work.

Paul describes the intended outcome: "till we all come to the unity of the faith and of the knowledge of the Son of God, to a perfect man, to the measure of the stature of the fullness of Christ."

This goal is both individual and corporate. Each person should grow toward spiritual maturity, but the entire body should also function with unity and effectiveness. Reliable messengers aren't developed in isolation—they're formed through healthy community relationships.

The phrase "measure of the stature of the fullness of Christ" sets the standard for spiritual development. We're not trying to become better versions of ourselves—we're being transformed to reflect Christ's character and ministry.

Paul contrasts mature believers with spiritual children who are "tossed to and fro and carried about with every wind of doctrine." Reliable messengers have developed enough spiritual maturity to recognize false teaching, maintain stability during difficulties, and help others grow rather than being constant consumers of ministry themselves.

"Speaking the truth in love, we will grow to become in every respect the mature body of him who is the head, that is, Christ." This beautiful description shows the church functioning as God intended—every part working together, supporting one another, and growing in love. Reliable messengers aren't independent operators but interdependent members of a functioning body.

Practical implications emerge for everyone. **For leaders:** Your primary job isn't to do all the ministry but to develop others who can do ministry. Success is measured not by how indispensable you are but by how effectively you've equipped others to serve.

For members: You're not meant to be a passive consumer of religious services but an active participant in God's work. Your spiritual growth should lead to greater capacity to serve others.

For churches: Evaluate your programs and structures based on whether they equip people for ministry or just provide religious entertainment. The goal is developing contributors, not just gathering consumers.

Paul uses the phrase "till we all come to..." indicating that this development continues throughout life. We never graduate from needing to be equipped, and we should always be involved in equipping others.

This lifelong perspective keeps us humble (we still need development) and motivated (we can always grow in effectiveness). It also means that equipping others isn't something we do only after we've "arrived"—it's part of our own growth process.

Living It Out

Reflection Questions:

1. How are you currently being equipped for more effective service as God's messenger?

2. What role do you play in equipping others—are you primarily receiving or giving at this stage of your development?

3. How does your church measure success—by how well leaders perform or by how effectively members are equipped?

Weekly Challenge: Identify one way you can contribute to the equipping process this week—either by seeking to be equipped or by helping equip someone else for more effective service.

Implementation Ideas:

- Assess your spiritual gifts and look for ways to use them in equipping others.

- Seek out training opportunities that will increase your effectiveness as God's messenger.

- Look for ways to help your church focus on equipping rather than just performing.

- Remember that being equipped is a lifelong process that involves both receiving and giving.

The Three Core Values

WEEK 28

LEARNING GOD'S WORD - VALUE 1

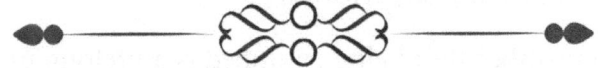

Psalm 119:97-104 (NLT) - Oh, how I love your instructions! I think about them all day long. Your commands make me wiser than my enemies, for they are my constant guide.

Etty Hillesum was a young Jewish woman confined to a Nazi transit camp in the Netherlands in 1943, waiting for transport to Auschwitz. In the midst of unimaginable horror, Hillesum made an extraordinary decision: she would spend part of each day copying passages from the Bible and other spiritual texts into a small notebook. Fellow prisoners thought she was wasting precious time and energy. But Hillesum understood something profound: "In the most degrading circumstances, when everything human seemed to be stripped away, the words I had hidden in my heart were the one thing they could never take from me. Those ancient texts became more real to me than the barbed wire around us."

The psalmist's passionate declaration in Psalm 119 reveals what it means to truly learn God's Word: "Oh, how I love Your instructions! I think about them all day long." The first value of reliable messengers is a commitment to learning God's Word through regular, prayerful study. This isn't casual Bible reading or academic study—it's the passionate pursuit of knowing God through His revealed truth.

Learning God's Word begins with understanding its nature. "All Scripture is given by inspiration of God." The word "inspiration" (*theopneustos*) literally means "God-breathed," indicating that Scripture is direct communication from God to humanity.

This divine origin sets the Bible apart from all other books. While human authors wrote using their personalities and styles, the Holy Spirit superintended the process to ensure that what they wrote was exactly what God wanted to communicate. This makes Scripture uniquely authoritative and reliable.

The psalmist doesn't describe duty or obligation—he declares love: "Oh, how I love Your law!" This emotional connection to Scripture transforms Bible study from drudgery into delight. When you genuinely love God's Word, you approach it with anticipation rather than obligation.

This love develops through experience. As you discover how Scripture speaks to your circumstances, provides wisdom for decisions, and reveals God's character, your appreciation deepens into genuine affection.

"It is my meditation all the day... Your testimonies are my meditation." The Hebrew word for meditation (*hagah*) means to mutter, murmur, or ponder deeply—like a cow chewing its cud. It suggests returning repeatedly to God's Word throughout the day, reflecting on its meaning and implications.

This constant engagement transforms how you think and respond to life situations. Instead of reacting based on emotions or cultural assumptions, you begin filtering experiences through biblical truth.

The psalmist claims to be wiser than enemies, more understanding than teachers, and more insightful than elders.

This isn't arrogance but testimony to Scripture's power to provide wisdom that surpasses human knowledge.

Wiser than enemies: God's Word provides strategic insight that enables you to navigate opposition and conflict with divine wisdom. **More understanding than teachers:** While human instruction is valuable, Scripture provides understanding that transcends even excellent teaching. **More than the ancients:** Accumulated human wisdom, while respectable, cannot match the timeless truth found in God's Word.

Here's a crucial connection: "I understand more than the ancients, because I keep Your precepts." Understanding and obedience are inseparably linked. You don't fully understand Scripture until you apply it, and you can't apply it effectively without understanding it.

"How sweet are Your words to my taste, sweeter than honey to my mouth!" The psalmist describes developing spiritual taste buds that find God's Word delicious. What once seemed difficult or boring becomes satisfying and enjoyable.

"Through Your precepts I get understanding; therefore I hate every false way." Scripture doesn't just provide information—it develops moral discernment that enables you to recognize and reject deception.

Practical aspects of learning God's Word include developing consistency, combining reading with reflection, practicing what you learn, and cultivating love for Scripture. Common obstacles include time pressure, information overload, perceived lack of relevance, and inconsistent application.

As Scripture transforms your understanding and character, you naturally become able to help others learn and apply biblical truth. The psalmist's superior wisdom enabled him to guide others toward God's ways.

Living It Out

Reflection Questions:

1. How would you honestly assess your current love for God's Word—is it genuine delight or dutiful obligation?

2. How do you currently practice "meditation all the day" on Scripture you've read?

3. In what ways has learning God's Word given you wisdom that surpasses conventional thinking?

Weekly Challenge: Choose one verse or passage from your Bible reading this week and practice "meditation all the day"—return to it repeatedly, thinking about its meaning and application throughout your daily activities.

Implementation Ideas:

- Develop a system for reviewing and reflecting on Scripture throughout the day.

- Start keeping a journal of insights and applications from your Bible reading.

- Practice explaining biblical truths to others to deepen your own understanding.

- Ask God to give you genuine love for His Word, not just discipline to read it.

WEEK 29

LOVING GOD'S WORD - VALUE 2

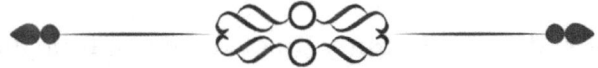

Mark *12:28-31 (ESV) - "Which commandment is the most important of all?" Jesus answered, "The most important is, 'Hear, O Israel: The Lord our God, the Lord is one. And you shall love the Lord your God with all your heart and with all your soul and with all your mind and with all your strength.' The second is this: 'You shall love your neighbor as yourself.'"*

(Story with Representative Practice) George Washington Carver, the renowned scientist who revolutionized agriculture in the American South, had an unusual practice. Each morning before entering his laboratory, he would walk through the woods around Tuskegee Institute, praying and reading his Bible. When asked about this habit, he explained that he needed to start each day by loving God with all his heart, soul, mind, and strength so he could love others through his scientific work. Carver understood that loving God's Word isn't just intellectual appreciation—it's wholehearted devotion that transforms how we live and serve.

The second value of reliable messengers moves beyond learning God's Word to loving God's Word by making love the highest priority of life. Jesus identified this as the greatest commandment, and reliable messengers organize their entire lives around this central commitment.

Jesus' quotation of the *Shema* emphasizes that loving God involves our entire being—heart, soul, mind, and strength. This isn't partial devotion or compartmentalized religion—it's total life integration around the priority of loving God.

Heart: The emotional center of our being. Loving God with all your heart means your deepest affections, desires, and feelings are oriented toward Him. **Soul:** The core of your identity and will. Loving God with all your soul means your fundamental choices and life direction are determined by your commitment to Him. **Mind:** Your intellectual capacity and thought patterns. Loving God with all your mind means your thinking is shaped by God's truth. **Strength:** Your physical energy and resources. Loving God with all your strength means your body, time, talents, and possessions are used in service to Him.

"The second is like it: 'You shall love your neighbor as yourself.'" Jesus connects these two commandments because authentic love for God always produces genuine love for people. You can't truly love the God you can't see while failing to love the people you can see.

This connection is crucial for reliable messengers. Our effectiveness in representing God to others flows directly from our love for God and our love for those we serve. People can detect whether our ministry comes from genuine love or from duty, ambition, or other motives.

When you love God deeply, His Word becomes more than a source of information—it becomes communication from your beloved. You read Scripture not just to learn facts but to hear His voice, understand His heart, and discover His will for your life.

This love-motivated approach to Scripture produces several important results. There's **hunger rather than duty**—you approach Bible study with anticipation. There's **personal application**—you look for how Scripture applies because you want to please the One you love. There's **obedience from affection**—you follow God's commands because you trust His love and wisdom. And there's **sharing with others**—you naturally want to share what you've discovered because people in love can't help talking about their beloved.

Loving God with all your heart, soul, mind, and strength doesn't eliminate difficulties—it provides motivation to persevere through them. When you truly love God, you're willing to make sacrifices, take risks, and endure hardships because you trust His character and purposes.

Here's what I've discovered: this love-motivated obedience differs significantly from duty-driven compliance. Duty may produce external conformity, but love produces joyful submission that persists even when no one is watching.

When your life is genuinely organized around loving God and loving others, people notice. Your relationships, decisions, priorities, and responses to difficulties all reflect your core commitments. This authentic love becomes a powerful testimony that validates your words about God's goodness.

Like any relationship, your love for God requires intentional nurturing. This involves spending time with Him, reflecting on His goodness, obeying His commands, and serving others in His name.

Jesus warned that we cannot serve both God and money, and this principle applies to any competing loyalty. When career ambitions, material desires, or personal comfort become more important than loving God, our effectiveness as reliable messengers is compromised.

While our capacity to love God comes from His love for us first, we still must choose to cultivate and express that love. Your love for God grows through attention and investment, and it diminishes through neglect and competing priorities.

The Great Commandment isn't just a nice religious ideal—it's the practical foundation for effective service as God's reliable messenger. When your life is genuinely organized around loving God and loving others, everything else finds its proper place and purpose.

Living It Out

Reflection Questions:

1. How would you honestly assess your love for God in each area—heart, soul, mind, and strength?

2. In what ways does your love for God motivate your obedience differently than duty or fear would?

3. How does your love for God express itself through practical love for the people around you?

Weekly Challenge: Identify one specific way you can demonstrate love for God through love for others this week. Look for someone who needs encouragement, help, or simply someone to notice them, and serve them as an expression of your love for God.

Implementation Ideas:

- Spend time each day reflecting on God's goodness and expressing gratitude for His love.

- Look for ways to serve others as a practical expression

of your love for God.

- Examine your priorities to identify any competing affections that might be displacing God.

- Practice thinking about how your daily activities can become expressions of love for God.

WEEK 30

LIVING GOD'S WORD - VALUE 3

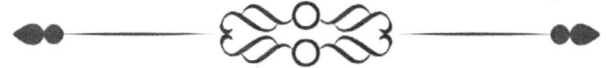

Matthew 28:18-20 (AMP) - Jesus came up and said to them, "All authority (all power of absolute rule) in heaven and on earth has been given to Me. Go therefore and make disciples of all the nations..."

In 1964, a young medical student named Paul Brand arrived in India to work at a leprosy hospital. For months, Brand studied everything he could about the disease—its progression, symptoms, and treatments. He became an expert on leprosy from a theoretical standpoint. But it wasn't until he actually began treating patients, performing surgeries, and developing new techniques for rehabilitation that his knowledge became truly meaningful. Brand later wrote, "I thought I understood leprosy when I could pass any exam about it. But I didn't really understand leprosy until I had held a patient's damaged hand in mine, looked into their eyes, and helped them regain function they thought was lost forever."

The third value of reliable messengers moves beyond learning and loving God's Word to living God's Word by taking biblical knowledge and love into active obedience through fulfilling the Great Commission.

"All authority in heaven and on earth has been given to Me." Before giving the commission, Jesus established His right to give it. His resurrection demonstrated His victory over death, sin, and Satan, proving His authority over every competing power.

This authority gives reliable messengers confidence to engage in seemingly impossible tasks. We're not attempting to fulfill the Great Commission through human wisdom, strength, or resources—we're operating under the authority of the One who has power over everything.

"Go therefore and make disciples of all the nations." The word "go" (*poreuomai*) can be translated "as you go," indicating that disciple-making should happen in the natural course of life, not just through special missionary trips.

"All the nations" (*panta ta ethne*) refers to all people groups, cultures, and communities. The Great Commission isn't limited to foreign missions—it includes reaching every distinct group of people wherever they are found.

"Baptizing them in the name of the Father and of the Son and of the Holy Spirit, teaching them to observe all things that I have commanded you." Making disciples isn't just getting people to make initial commitments to Christ—it's developing them into mature followers who obey His teachings.

Baptism is firstly a matter of obedience and represents public identification with Christ and the beginning of the Christian journey. **Teaching to observe** goes beyond information transfer to lifestyle transformation. The goal isn't just biblical knowledge but biblical obedience that produces Christ-like character and behavior.

"And lo, I am with you always, even to the end of the age." The same Jesus who has all authority promises to be with us as we fulfill His commission. His presence provides courage for difficult assignments, wisdom for complex situations, and power for supernatural results.

Living God's Word through the Great Commission requires practical commitment to evangelism, discipleship, church planting, and sending. The Great Commission begins where you are but extends to the ends of the earth. Reliable messengers understand that they have responsibilities both in their immediate sphere of influence and in the broader world.

Your family, workplace, neighborhood, and community represent your primary mission field. If you can't be an effective witness where people know you best, your ability to impact distant places is questionable. But you also have an obligation to pray for, support, and potentially participate in reaching people groups and geographic areas beyond your immediate context.

Here's the truth: living God's Word requires both being and going. Some people are called to go to distant places as missionaries, church planters, or humanitarian workers. Others are called to stay where they are and support those who go through prayer, financial support, and developing local ministry that prepares others for service.

When you make disciples who make disciples, your impact multiplies exponentially. Consider the mathematical difference: If you personally led one person to Christ every year for 40 years, you would reach 40 people. But if you discipled one person each year who discipled another person each year, you would impact over one billion people by the end of 40 years. Multiplication is far more powerful than addition.

While some people have specific calling to vocational ministry, every Christian is called to participate in fulfilling the Great Commission. Your role might be different from others, but you have a role. This might involve sharing your faith with friends, supporting missionaries, serving in outreach ministries, using professional skills in cross-cultural contexts, mentoring newer believers, or raising children who understand their missionary calling.

Living It Out

Reflection Questions:

1. How are you currently participating in fulfilling the Great Commission both locally and globally?

2. What specific people groups or geographic areas has God burdened your heart to pray for and potentially serve?

3. How can you move from learning and loving God's Word to living it more fully through disciple-making?

Weekly Challenge: Take one specific action this week toward fulfilling the Great Commission. Whether it's starting a spiritual conversation, supporting a missionary, serving in your community, or beginning to disciple someone, move from learning to living.

Implementation Ideas:

- Identify your role in the Great Commission and develop a personal mission statement.

- Look for natural opportunities to share your faith or serve others in Jesus' name.

- Support cross-cultural ministry through prayer, giving, or direct involvement.

- Find someone you can begin discipling or ask someone to disciple you.

Transformation Process

WEEK 31

INFORMATION TO TRANSFORMATION

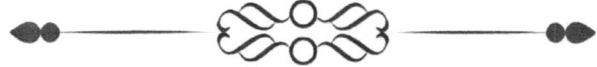

Romans 12:1-2 (ESV) - I appeal to you therefore, brothers, by the mercies of God, to present your bodies as a living sacrifice, holy and acceptable to God, which is your spiritual worship. Do not be conformed to this world, but be transformed by the renewal of your mind...

In 1901, Guglielmo Marconi successfully transmitted the first transatlantic radio signal—the letter "S" in Morse code sent from Cornwall, England to Newfoundland, Canada. The information traveled 2,100 miles in an instant, but receiving the signal wasn't enough. It had to be decoded, understood, and acted upon to be useful. Similarly, many believers are excellent at receiving spiritual information—sermons, Bible studies, books, and teachings—but struggle with the transformation process that turns information into life change.

The journey from information to transformation involves several crucial steps that reliable messengers must understand and experience.

"I appeal to you therefore, brothers, by the mercies of God, to present your bodies as a living sacrifice, holy and acceptable to God, which is your spiritual worship." Paul connects transformation to surrender, using language that would have been familiar to his readers from temple sacrifices.

A sacrifice is something given completely to God, no longer available for the giver's personal use. A "living sacrifice" is someone who has died to their own agenda while remaining alive to serve God's purposes. This complete surrender is the foundation for all genuine transformation.

Paul calls this surrender our "reasonable service" (*logikos latreia*), which means logical or rational worship. Transformation isn't based on emotional highs or mystical experiences—it's a logical response to understanding who God is and what He has done for us.

The "mercies of God" that motivate this surrender include everything Paul described in the first eleven chapters of Romans: justification, adoption, sanctification, and glorification. When you truly understand what God has done for you, complete surrender becomes the only reasonable response.

"Do not be conformed to this world." The word "conformed" (*suschematizo*) means to be pressed into a mold or shaped by external pressure. Paul warns against allowing the world's values, priorities, and methods to shape your thinking and behavior.

This conformity pressure is constant and subtle. Culture gradually shapes our attitudes toward money, relationships, success, entertainment, and values unless we actively resist. Reliable messengers must be intentionally counter-cultural, allowing God's truth to shape them instead of absorbing the world's patterns.

"But be transformed by the renewing of your mind." The word "transformed" (*metamorphoo*) is where we get "metamorphosis"—the process by which a caterpillar becomes a butterfly. This transformation is comprehensive, not just surface-level change.

Mind renewal involves several elements. There's **new information**—learning biblical truth that challenges wrong thinking patterns. There's **new interpretation**—understanding how to view circumstances through the lens of Scripture. There's **new imagination**—beginning to see possibilities that align with God's purposes. And there's **new integration**—connecting biblical truth to daily decisions until it becomes your natural way of processing life.

"That you may prove what is that good and acceptable and perfect will of God." The word "prove" (*dokimazo*) means to test and approve, like testing metals for purity. Renewed thinking enables you to recognize and choose God's will in specific situations.

Common barriers to transformation include information overload without application, emotional resistance to surrender, social pressure to conform, and impatience with the process. Many people accumulate biblical knowledge without allowing it to change their behavior. They become experts at discussing theology while remaining unchanged in character and lifestyle.

Like physical fitness, spiritual transformation requires consistent effort over time. Small daily choices to think and act according to God's truth gradually reshape your character and automatic responses.

As you experience genuine change through applying God's truth to your life, you develop authentic testimony about His transforming power. People are far more likely to be influenced by someone who has obviously been changed by what they're

133

representing.

While surrender and mind renewal are personal choices, transformation happens best in community with other believers who can encourage, challenge, and model spiritual growth. Iron sharpens iron, and we need relationships with people who are also committed to being transformed by God's truth.

While we cooperate with the transformation process through surrender and mind renewal, the actual change is produced by the Holy Spirit working in us. This means transformation is both supernatural and natural—supernatural in its source and power, natural in its expression through human choices and actions.

Living It Out

Reflection Questions:

1. In what areas of your life are you still being conformed to the world's patterns rather than being transformed by God's truth?

2. How would you assess your current journey from information to transformation—are you gaining knowledge faster than you're applying it?

3. What specific practices help you move from learning biblical truth to experiencing life change through it?

Weekly Challenge: Choose one area where you have good biblical information but haven't experienced transformation, and take specific steps this week to apply what you know. Focus on mind renewal and practical obedience rather than just learning more information.

Implementation Ideas:

- Identify specific worldly patterns you need to resist and biblical alternatives you need to embrace.

- Develop practices that help you apply biblical truth to daily decisions.

- Find accountability partners who will help you move from information to transformation.

- Remember that transformation is a process that requires patience and consistency.

The E5 Process

WEEK 32

THE E5 PROCESS: ENCOUNTER

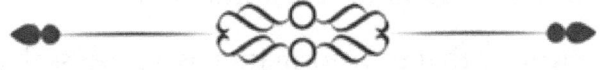

Acts 9:3-6 (ESV) - Now as he went on his way, he approached Damascus, and suddenly a light from heaven shone around him. And falling to the ground, he heard a voice saying to him, "Saul, Saul, why are you persecuting me?"

In 1945, a shell-shocked American soldier named Louis Zamperini sat in his apartment in California, drowning his war memories in alcohol and rage. His life was falling apart—his marriage was crumbling, he was plagued by nightmares, and he could barely function in civilian society. His wife Cynthia begged him to attend a Billy Graham crusade with her. Zamperini reluctantly agreed, planning to leave after a few minutes. But as Graham spoke about God's love and forgiveness, something extraordinary happened. Zamperini later described it: "Suddenly, it was like a dam burst inside me. All the hatred, all the anger, all the pain I'd been carrying—it was like God reached down and lifted it off my shoulders in an instant."

At high noon on the road to Damascus, a brilliant light more intense than the Syrian sun suddenly surrounded Saul of Tarsus. The future apostle Paul fell to the ground, blinded by the radiance and shaken by a voice asking, "Saul, Saul, why are you persecuting Me?" This encounter with the risen Christ changed everything—Saul's beliefs, identity, mission, and eternal destiny.

The first E—Encounter—represents the initial collision between human life and divine reality. While not everyone experiences this as dramatically as Paul, every reliable messenger must have a genuine encounter with God that establishes the foundation for everything that follows.

Encounters are initiated by God, not manufactured by humans. Paul wasn't seeking a spiritual experience when the light surrounded him. He was actively opposing Christianity, confident in his religious convictions. God interrupted his journey with an undeniable divine encounter.

This pattern appears throughout Scripture. Moses was caring for sheep when he encountered God in the burning bush. Isaiah was in the temple when he saw the Lord high and lifted up. Mary was going about her daily life when the angel announced God's plan.

While we can position ourselves to encounter God through prayer, worship, and Scripture study, we cannot manufacture genuine encounters. They are gifts from God's grace, given according to His sovereign timing and purposes.

Paul's encounter included several revelations about God's nature. The blazing light revealed God's glory and holiness. The voice speaking his name demonstrated God's personal knowledge and concern. The question "Why are you persecuting Me?" revealed that attacking Christians meant attacking Christ Himself.

Every genuine encounter with God includes some revelation of His character that challenges our previous understanding. We discover aspects of His love, holiness, power, or wisdom that we hadn't fully grasped before.

The light that revealed God's glory also exposed Paul's spiritual blindness. The voice that spoke with authority revealed Paul's rebellion against God's purposes. The encounter forced Paul to confront the reality that his religious activities were actually opposition to God's will.

God didn't just reveal Himself to Paul—He spoke to him. The conversation was brief but life-changing: "I am Jesus, whom you are persecuting... Rise and go into the city, and you will be told what you must do."

Paul's encounter ended with clear instructions. He could have ignored these instructions, argued with the voice, or rationalized the experience away. Instead, he obeyed immediately, even though it meant abandoning his previous mission and facing an uncertain future.

Paul's encounter disrupted his travel plans, his career, his relationships, and his future. He went from being a rising star in Judaism to being temporarily blind and dependent on others for guidance.

Here's what I've observed: God's encounters with humans often involve disruption because we naturally resist change. Divine encounters create necessary disruption that opens us to new possibilities.

While Paul's encounter was intensely personal, it wasn't private. His traveling companions witnessed the light and heard the voice, though they didn't fully understand what was happening. Later, Paul would share his encounter story repeatedly as part of his testimony.

Not all encounters are dramatic. While Paul's was spectacular, many divine encounters are quieter but equally transformational. The key isn't the dramatic nature of the experience but its authentic, life-changing impact.

Paul's encounter revealed not just his need for salvation but his calling to be an apostle to the Gentiles. Your encounter with God may reveal your specific calling, or it may establish the foundation for calling that becomes clear later.

Paul's initial encounter led to baptism, immediate preaching, and eventually to ongoing revelation and ministry. One encounter with God typically creates an appetite for ongoing relationship rather than satisfying spiritual curiosity.

Living It Out

Reflection Questions:

1. How would you describe your personal encounter(s) with the living God?

2. What aspects of God's character became more real to you through your divine encounter?

3. How did your encounter with God disrupt your previous plans and create a new direction for your life?

Weekly Challenge: If you haven't experienced a clear encounter with God, position yourself this week through prayer and Scripture study to meet with Him. If you have had such an encounter, share your story with someone who needs to hear about God's personal interest in their life.

Implementation Ideas:

- Spend time reflecting on and perhaps writing about your personal encounter with God.

- Look for opportunities to share your encounter story as encouragement to others.

- Position yourself for ongoing encounters through worship, prayer, and Scripture meditation.

- Remember that encounters are beginnings, not destinations—they launch you into the rest of the E5 process.

WEEK 33

THE E5 PROCESS: EXPERIENCE

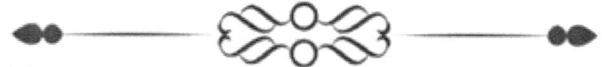

Luke 24:32 (AMP) - They said to one another, "Were not our hearts burning within us while He was talking with us on the road and opening the Scriptures to us?"

(Story with Representative Reflection) In 1962, astronaut John Glenn became the first American to orbit Earth. As his spacecraft, Friendship 7, soared 162 miles above the planet, Glenn experienced something no amount of training had prepared him for. "I had studied photographs of Earth taken from space," he later recalled. "I had memorized every detail of what I was supposed to see. But when I actually witnessed that first sunrise from orbit—watching the sun emerge from behind the curved horizon of our blue planet—I was overwhelmed. The difference between knowing about Earth from space and actually experiencing Earth from space was like the difference between reading about love and falling in love."

Two discouraged disciples walked the dusty road from Jerusalem to Emmaus, their hopes shattered by Jesus' crucifixion. A stranger joined their journey, and as He explained the Scriptures, something remarkable happened: "Were not our hearts burning within us while He was talking with us on the road and opening the Scriptures to us?"

Experience moves beyond the initial encounter to develop a personal, ongoing relationship with God that engages your whole being—mind, heart, emotions, and will.

The disciples' "burning hearts" represent emotional response to spiritual truth. While encounters can be sudden and dramatic, experiences develop over time as you learn to recognize and respond to God's presence in your daily life.

This emotional dimension is important because humans are emotional beings. While we shouldn't base our faith solely on feelings, an authentic relationship with God naturally produces emotional responses—joy, peace, conviction, gratitude, love, and sometimes grief over sin.

Notice that the disciples' hearts burned specifically "while He opened the Scriptures to us." Their experience wasn't based on mystical feelings divorced from biblical truth. Instead, it came through understanding God's Word more clearly.

Reliable messengers learn to experience God primarily through Scripture. As you read, study, and meditate on biblical truth, the Holy Spirit makes it come alive in your heart and mind. Passages that once seemed like ancient history become personal messages from God to your current situation.

The disciples didn't immediately recognize that their traveling companion was Jesus, but they recognized that something significant was happening. They had spiritual sensitivity that enabled them to detect God's presence even when they couldn't fully explain it.

Developing this spiritual sensitivity is crucial for reliable messengers. You learn to recognize God's voice, sense His leading, and detect spiritual significance in circumstances that others might view as merely natural events.

When the stranger explained "in all the Scriptures the things concerning Himself," He wasn't giving abstract theological lectures. He was showing them how all of Scripture pointed to the Messiah they thought had failed them. This personal application transformed their despair into hope.

Your experience of God should include increasing ability to see how biblical truth applies to your specific circumstances, relationships, challenges, and opportunities. Scripture becomes personally relevant rather than just historically interesting.

The disciples' recognition of Jesus was gradual. Their hearts burned during the journey, but they didn't realize who their companion was until He broke bread with them. Then "their eyes were opened and they knew Him."

Most people's experience of God develops progressively rather than all at once. You may sense God's presence or understand His truth in increasing measure over time. This gradual process requires patience and persistence, but it produces deeper, more stable spiritual maturity.

Even after recognizing Jesus, the disciples were left with questions. Why hadn't they recognized Him earlier? Why did He disappear immediately after revealing Himself? Experience of God includes both wonderful clarity and continued mystery.

The disciples immediately returned to Jerusalem to share their experience with the other believers. When they arrived, they found others who had similar experiences: "The Lord is risen indeed, and has appeared to Simon!"

Authentic spiritual experience seeks validation and fellowship with other believers. While your relationship with God is personal, it shouldn't be private. Other mature Christians can help you understand and interpret your spiritual experiences.

Experience can be hindered by unconfessed sin, busy

lifestyle, intellectual pride, and past disappointments. Sin creates barriers to experiencing God's presence. A lifestyle filled with constant activity makes it difficult to develop spiritual sensitivity. Some people try to approach God purely through intellectual study while neglecting the heart. And previous spiritual disappointments can make people cautious about opening their hearts to experience God deeply.

The disciples' burning hearts and recognition of Jesus prepared them to return to Jerusalem, where they would soon experience Pentecost and become bold witnesses. Experience of God isn't an end in itself—it prepares you for the exchange, endeavor, and encouragement that follow.

When you've genuinely experienced God's presence, guidance, and love, you have an authentic testimony to share with others. People can argue with your theology, but they can't argue with your experience.

Living It Out

Reflection Questions:

1. How would you describe your ongoing experience of God's presence in your daily life?

2. When has your "heart burned within you" as you've engaged with Scripture or worship?

3. What factors in your life currently help or hinder your ability to experience God personally?

Weekly Challenge: Create space this week for experiencing God more fully. Spend extended time in Scripture and prayer, looking for ways your heart can be "burned within you" as He opens His truth to your understanding.

Implementation Ideas:

- Develop practices that help you slow down and become aware of God's presence.

- Keep a journal of how you experience God through Scripture, prayer, and circumstances.

- Share your spiritual experiences with trusted believers for validation and encouragement.

- Look for ways to remove barriers that prevent you from experiencing God more fully.

WEEK 34

THE E5 PROCESS: EXCHANGE

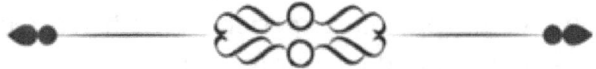

Galatians 2:20 (ESV) - I have been crucified with Christ. It is no longer I who live, but Christ who lives in me. And the life I now live in the flesh I live by faith in the Son of God, who loved me and gave himself for me.

On October 31, 1517, Martin Luther nailed his 95 Theses to the door of the Castle Church in Wittenberg, challenging the practice of selling indulgences. But Luther's public protest flowed from a personal exchange that had transformed his own life. He had discovered that salvation couldn't be purchased, earned, or merited—it was received by faith alone as a gift from God's grace. This exchange of his works-based righteousness for Christ's perfect righteousness changed not only Luther's eternal destiny but launched the Protestant Reformation.

The Exchange represents the crucial turning point where encounter and experience lead to fundamental life change. It's the decision to trade your old life, priorities, and methods for God's new life, priorities, and methods.

Paul's description in Galatians 2:20 reveals the depth of this exchange: "I have been crucified with Christ; it is no longer I who live, but Christ lives in me." This isn't just behavioral modification or adopting new habits—it's identity transformation. Paul's former identity as a self-righteous

Pharisee died, and his new identity became "one in whom Christ lives."

Notice Paul's use of past tense: "I have been crucified." This wasn't an ongoing struggle or gradual process—it was a definitive decision. At some point, Paul chose to consider his old life dead and his new life alive in Christ.

While this decision may need to be renewed and reinforced regularly, it begins with a conscious choice to exchange your agenda for God's agenda, your limitations for His provisions, and your methods for His wisdom.

The exchange affects both spiritual and practical dimensions. There's **spiritual exchange**—trading your sin for His forgiveness, your weakness for His strength, your fear for His peace. And there's **practical exchange**—trading your career ambitions for His calling, your financial priorities for His stewardship principles, your relationship choices for His guidance.

The word "exchange" implies trading something of value for something of greater value. This isn't about giving up worthless things—it's about surrendering good things for better things, or even best things for God's things.

Abraham exchanged the security of familiar surroundings for God's promise of unknown blessings. Moses exchanged the privileges of Pharaoh's house for identification with God's people. Paul exchanged his impressive religious credentials for "the surpassing worth of knowing Christ Jesus my Lord."

After encountering and experiencing God, you may still try to serve Him using your old methods, abilities, and resources. The exchange includes surrendering your approaches to problems and relationships in favor of God's wisdom.

This often means choosing biblical principles over cultural norms, spiritual solutions over purely practical ones, and eternal perspectives over temporary advantages.

When you exchange your agenda for God's agenda, you begin to want what He wants, value what He values, and pursue what He's pursuing. This unity of purpose is the foundation for effective service as a reliable messenger.

Instead of asking God to bless your plans, you begin asking how you can participate in His plans. Instead of seeking God's help with your priorities, you surrender your priorities to discover His.

Exchange often involves specific areas like financial priorities, relational patterns, professional goals, and personal habits. Each area requires conscious decision to exchange worldly approaches for godly ones.

When Paul describes being "crucified with Christ," he doesn't mean losing his personality or unique abilities. Throughout his ministry, Paul remained intellectually gifted, passionately committed, and strategically minded. The exchange refined and redirected these qualities rather than eliminating them.

Here's the truth: God doesn't want to make you into someone else—He wants to make you into the best version of yourself, aligned with His purposes and empowered by His Spirit.

One of the most difficult aspects of exchange is surrendering your timeline for God's timeline. You may feel ready for certain opportunities or frustrated by delays in seeing results from your service.

The exchange includes trusting God's timing, even when it doesn't make sense from a human perspective. His timeline often involves more preparation, different opportunities, or unexpected delays that serve purposes you can't see immediately.

When you exchange your life for Christ's life in you, you become accountable to Him for how you use the abilities, resources, and opportunities He provides. This accountability isn't burdensome—it's liberating because it clarifies priorities and decision-making.

Jesus warned that following Him might cost relationships, comfort, or worldly success. But He also promised that those who lose their lives for His sake will find them.

The exchange may involve short-term sacrifices, but it always produces long-term benefits—both in this life and eternity. Peace, purpose, joy, and eternal significance far outweigh temporary losses.

Once you've exchanged your life for Christ's life in you, you're prepared for the endeavor phase—actually doing the work He's called you to do. Without the exchange, you might attempt to serve God using your old methods and motivations, which limits effectiveness.

While the initial decision to exchange your life for Christ's life can be a crisis moment, living out that exchange is an ongoing process. You'll regularly face decisions about whether to operate from your old patterns or your new identity in Christ.

When people see that you've genuinely exchanged worldly pursuits for spiritual ones, your testimony carries authenticity. This authentic exchange becomes one of your most powerful tools as a reliable messenger.

Living It Out

Reflection Questions:

1. What specific areas of your life still need to be exchanged—surrendered to God's control and purposes?

2. How does living from your new identity in Christ differ from trying to serve God with your old methods?

3. What timeline or outcome are you struggling to surrender to God's wisdom?

Weekly Challenge: Identify one significant area where you've been holding back from complete exchange. This week, make a conscious decision to surrender it to God's control, trusting Him with the outcomes.

Implementation Ideas:

- Write out what you're exchanging (surrendering) and what you're receiving from Christ.

- Practice "death and resurrection" thinking—daily acknowledge what needs to die and what Christ wants to bring alive.

- Find accountability for areas where you struggle to maintain the exchange.

- Remember that exchange is both a crisis decision and an ongoing process of surrender.

WEEK 35

THE E5 PROCESS: ENDEAVOR

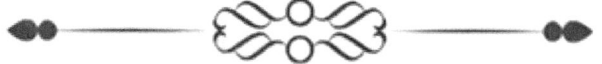

Philippians 2:12-13 (AMP) - So then, my dear ones... continue to work out your salvation [that is, cultivate it, bring it to full effect, actively pursue spiritual maturity] with awe-inspired fear and trembling... For it is [not your strength, but it is] God who is effectively at work in you...

(Story with Representative Reflection) In 1928, Scottish microbiologist Alexander Fleming returned to his London laboratory after a two-week vacation to find that one of his bacterial culture dishes had been contaminated by mold. Most scientists would have thrown away the ruined experiment and started over. But Fleming had encountered the wonders of scientific discovery, experienced the thrill of breakthrough research, and exchanged his comfortable routine for a passion to find new treatments for disease. Now came the moment of endeavor—would he discard this apparent failure or investigate further? Fleming chose to examine the contaminated dish and made a startling discovery: the mold had killed all the bacteria around it. Fleming later reflected, "I had been preparing for this moment my entire career, but preparation without action would have meant nothing."

After transformation through encounter, experience, and exchange, reliable messengers face the fourth E—Endeavor—where spiritual change produces practical action.

Paul's instruction to "work out your own salvation with awe-inspired fear and trembling" comes immediately after his description of Christ's incarnation and sacrifice. The working out is based on what God has already worked in, not an attempt to earn what hasn't been given.

This distinction is crucial for reliable messengers. Your endeavor should flow from your encounter, experience, and exchange with God, not be an attempt to earn His approval or prove your worth. You serve from acceptance, not for acceptance.

"For it is God who is effectively at work in you both to will and to work for His good pleasure." This paradox characterizes all effective spiritual endeavors—we work hard while depending completely on God's power.

This isn't passive waiting for God to do everything, nor is it exhausting self-effort. It's active cooperation with God's work in and through you. You apply maximum effort while maintaining complete dependence on His enablement.

The phrase "for His good pleasure" indicates that our endeavor should focus on what pleases God rather than what pleases us or impresses others. This requires ongoing discernment about which activities truly serve God's kingdom purposes.

Not all religious activity qualifies as godly endeavor. Some church work, ministry projects, and spiritual activities may be motivated by personal ambition, social pressure, or tradition rather than alignment with God's will.

Just as Jesus called Peter to launch out into the deep and let down his nets, God calls reliable messengers to attempt things that require faith and depend on His power for success.

This doesn't mean being reckless or presumptuous, but it does mean being willing to take calculated risks for kingdom purposes. Your encounter, experience, and exchange with God should increase your willingness to attempt things that are impossible without His help.

The exchange process often reveals or clarifies your spiritual gifts—the specific ways God has equipped you to serve His purposes. Endeavor involves actively using these gifts rather than letting them remain dormant.

Some people discover their gifts through their endeavor—they try different forms of service and find that God blesses certain activities more than others. Others receive clear understanding of their gifts before they begin serving. Either way, endeavor involves putting your gifts to work.

Endeavor includes both individual elements (personal spiritual disciplines, lifestyle choices) and corporate elements (participation in church ministries, community service, evangelistic efforts). Both dimensions are important for balanced, effective service.

Paul's ministry included beatings, imprisonment, shipwrecks, and opposition from both religious and secular authorities. Yet he continued his endeavor because he understood that obstacles are normal parts of meaningful service.

Your endeavor will likely face obstacles as well—lack of resources, opposition from others, personal limitations, or circumstances beyond your control. Reliable messengers persist in their endeavor despite obstacles, trusting God to provide what's needed.

Effective endeavor doesn't just accomplish immediate tasks—it develops other people who can continue and expand the work. Paul's endeavor included training Timothy, Titus, and many others who would carry on his mission.

As you engage in endeavor, look for opportunities to involve others, teach them skills, and develop them for their own ministry calling. This multiplication approach extends your impact far beyond what you could accomplish individually.

While the call to endeavor is clear, the specific timing and methods require ongoing discernment. God may call you to wait for better timing, prepare more thoroughly, or use different approaches than you initially planned.

The demands of active service can drain your spiritual reserves unless you maintain consistent practices of prayer, Scripture study, worship, and fellowship with other believers.

Many people start their endeavor with great enthusiasm but burn out because they neglect the spiritual practices that sustain long-term service. Like athletes who must maintain physical conditioning, reliable messengers must maintain spiritual conditioning.

As you step out in faith and see God work through your efforts, you experience the encouragement that comes from participating in His purposes. This encouragement, the fifth E, provides motivation to continue and often leads to new cycles of encounter, experience, exchange, and endeavor.

Meaningful endeavor often costs time, energy, money, and comfort. But here's what I've discovered: it produces deep satisfaction that comes from knowing your life is making an eternal difference. This satisfaction is far greater than what comes from purely selfish pursuits.

Living It Out

Reflection Questions:

1. How is God currently calling you to endeavor—to put feet to your faith through active service?

2. What obstacles or fears have been preventing you from fully engaging in the endeavor God has for you?

3. How are you balancing human effort with dependence on God's empowerment in your current service?

Weekly Challenge: Take one specific step this week toward the endeavor God has placed on your heart. Whether it's starting a new ministry, having a difficult conversation, or serving someone in need, move from planning to action.

Implementation Ideas:

*   Identify your spiritual gifts and look for ways to use them in service to others.

*   Start with small acts of obedience that build confidence for larger endeavors.

*   Find others who share your sense of calling and can work with you in endeavor.

*   Maintain spiritual disciplines that sustain you for long-term service.

WEEK 36

THE E5 PROCESS: ENCOURAGEMENT

1 Thessalonians 5:9-11 (ESV) - For God has not destined us for wrath, but to obtain salvation through our Lord Jesus Christ, who died for us so that whether we are awake or asleep we might live with him. Therefore encourage one another and build one another up, just as you are doing.

In 1953, New Zealand beekeeper Edmund Hillary and his Sherpa guide Tenzing Norgay became the first people to reach the summit of Mount Everest. But Hillary later said the moment that defined the expedition wasn't standing on top of the world's highest peak—it was what happened during their descent. As they made their way down, they encountered other climbing teams who had failed in their attempts. Instead of simply passing by, Hillary and Norgay stopped to share their oxygen, their food, and most importantly, their story. Hillary recalled, "We told them exactly how we did it. We showed them the route, warned them about the dangers, and assured them it was possible because we had just done it." Over the following years, many of those climbers returned to Everest and successfully reached the summit themselves.

Barnabas earned his name, which means "Son of Encouragement," not through a single dramatic act but through a lifestyle of seeing potential in others and helping them realize it. He encouraged Saul when the disciples feared the former persecutor. He encouraged John Mark when Paul considered him unreliable. He encouraged the believers in Antioch when they needed leadership and teaching.

Encouragement represents both the culmination and the continuation of the E5 process. It's the fruit that comes from encounter, experience, exchange, and endeavor, but it's also the catalyst that launches others into their own transformational journey.

When you've genuinely encountered God, experienced His presence, exchanged your life for His purposes, and engaged in faithful endeavor, encouragement becomes your natural response to others. You can't help but want to share what you've discovered and help others experience the same transformation.

This isn't forced or artificial encouragement—it's the authentic overflow of a life that has been changed by God's goodness. People can sense the difference between genuine encouragement and empty positivity.

Like Barnabas seeing apostolic potential in the feared Saul, encouragement looks beyond current limitations to future possibilities. Reliable messengers learn to see people through God's eyes, recognizing that He can transform anyone just as He transformed them.

Paul's instruction to "encourage one another and build each other up" is accompanied by practical methods. Effective encouragement includes concrete actions that actually help people grow and succeed. This might involve sharing resources, connecting people with opportunities, providing practical support, teaching skills, or praying specifically for others' needs.

When you encourage others to begin their own E5 journey, your influence extends far beyond what you could accomplish individually. Each person you encourage may encourage others, creating exponential impact across generations.

Barnabas didn't just give Saul encouraging words—he vouched for him with the apostles, traveled with him on missionary journeys, and invested years in his development. Real encouragement often requires significant investment of time, energy, and resources.

When Barnabas chose to give John Mark a second chance after his failure, it cost him his ministry partnership with Paul. Sometimes encouraging others requires taking risks or facing criticism from people who don't share your vision for someone's potential.

The person you encourage may eventually become more effective than you are. John Mark, whom Barnabas encouraged despite his early failure, eventually wrote the Gospel of Mark and became valuable even to Paul. True encouragement celebrates others' success rather than being threatened by it.

The E5 process reveals that people need different types of encouragement depending on their stage of development. Those needing encounter need encouragement to seek God. Those processing experience need encouragement to trust their spiritual senses. Those facing exchange need encouragement to surrender completely. Those engaged in endeavor need encouragement to persist despite obstacles. And those providing encouragement need encouragement themselves to continue investing.

Barnabas wasn't known for one encouraging act but for a pattern of encouraging behavior. He made encouragement his trademark characteristic. Reliable messengers develop this same lifestyle of consistently looking for ways to build up others.

One of the remarkable outcomes of the E5 process is that encouragement becomes a source of joy rather than a burden. When you see someone you've encouraged succeed in their calling, experience spiritual growth, or overcome significant obstacles, their success becomes a source of deep satisfaction.

While encouragement builds people up, its ultimate purpose is to direct them toward God rather than toward the encourager. Effective encouragement helps people see God's work in their lives, trust His promises for their future, and depend on His strength for their challenges.

As you encourage others and they begin their own E5 journey, you often find yourself launched into new cycles as well. Their growth and success may open new opportunities for your own encounter, experience, exchange, and endeavor.

This cyclical nature of the E5 process means that spiritual growth and ministry effectiveness continue throughout life. Each completed cycle prepares you for greater challenges and opportunities in subsequent cycles.

Living It Out

Reflection Questions:

1. Who has served as an encourager in your life, helping you through various stages of the E5 process?

2. How is God calling you to encourage others who are at different stages of spiritual development?

3. What prevents you from being more intentional about encouraging others in their spiritual growth and

ministry calling?

Weekly Challenge: Identify someone who needs encouragement and provide specific, practical help this week. Look for ways to help them see their potential and take next steps in their spiritual development.

Implementation Ideas:

- Develop eyes to see potential in people that others might overlook.

- Practice giving specific, truthful encouragement rather than general praise.

- Look for practical ways to support people during challenging seasons.

- Celebrate others' successes and growth as enthusiastically as you would your own.

The E4 Leadership Model

WEEK 37

THE E4 LEADERSHIP MODEL: ENGAGE

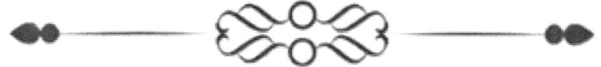

John 1:35-42 (ESV) - The next day again John was standing with two of his disciples, and he looked at Jesus as he walked by and said, "Behold, the Lamb of God!" The two disciples heard him say this, and they followed Jesus. Jesus turned and saw them following and said to them, "What are you seeking?"

In 1987, Howard Schultz visited Italy and experienced something that would transform not just his career but American culture itself. In Italian coffee bars, he witnessed baristas who knew their customers by name, conversations that lingered over espresso, and community connections that transcended mere transactions. The coffee wasn't just a product—it was a platform for engagement. When Schultz returned to America and eventually acquired Starbucks, he didn't just sell coffee; he created what he called "the third place"—a space between work and home where meaningful connections could happen.

This principle of engagement forms the foundation of the E4 Leadership Model. Jesus demonstrated this perfectly in His interaction with His first disciples. Notice how engagement works—it's personal, intentional, and transformative.

When Jesus turned and saw the two disciples following Him, He didn't see potential statistics or ministry resources. He saw individuals with names, stories, and destinies. His first words weren't a recruitment pitch but a question: "What are you seeking?" This wasn't information-gathering; Jesus already knew their hearts. It was an invitation—an opportunity for them to articulate their spiritual hunger.

When the disciples asked where Jesus was staying, they weren't requesting His address. They were expressing a desire for more than a passing encounter. Jesus' response—"Come and you will see"—invited them into His life, not just His teaching. They "stayed with him that day," spending unhurried time that allowed genuine connection to develop.

Andrew's first response after spending time with Jesus was to find his brother Simon. He didn't distribute flyers or make announcements. He shared a personal testimony: "We have found the Messiah." This personal engagement—one person inviting another into an encounter with Jesus—remains the most effective form of evangelism.

When Jesus looked at Simon, He saw more than a rough fisherman. "You are Simon... You shall be called Cephas (Peter)." Jesus engaged with who Simon was while prophetically declaring who he would become. This is the essence of transformative engagement—meeting people where they are while calling them to who they can be.

The E4 Leadership Model follows this pattern: **Engage** (create meaningful connections), **Equip** (provide tools, knowledge, and skills), **Empower** (release authority and responsibility), and **Encourage** (sustain momentum through support).

Engagement is the crucial first step because without genuine connection, the other elements become mere programs rather than transformative relationships. You can't effectively equip someone you haven't engaged. You can't empower someone who doesn't trust you. You can't encourage someone who doesn't believe you care.

In our distracted age, reliable messengers must be intentional about creating space for genuine engagement. This might mean remembering names and stories, asking questions that invite deeper conversation, creating environments where people feel safe to be authentic, following up on previous conversations, and being fully present rather than mentally multitasking.

Living It Out

Reflection Questions:

1. How well do you engage with people before trying to equip or correct them?

2. What prevents you from deeper engagement with those God has placed in your life?

3. Who in your sphere of influence needs you to see their potential and speak it into existence?

Weekly Challenge: This week, practice the ministry of engagement. Choose three people and engage them meaningfully—ask about their stories, listen without agenda, and look for opportunities to affirm their potential. Don't try to fix, teach, or correct. Simply engage.

Implementation Ideas:

- Schedule coffee or lunch with someone without any agenda except connection.

- Practice remembering and using people's names in conversation.

- Ask follow-up questions that show you remember previous conversations.

- Create margin in your schedule for unhurried conversations.

- Look for the potential in people and speak it out when appropriate.

WEEK 38

THE E4 LEADERSHIP MODEL: EQUIP

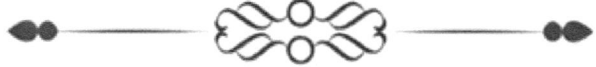

Luke 9:1-6 (ESV) - And he called the twelve together and gave them power and authority over all demons and to cure diseases, and he sent them out to proclaim the kingdom of God and to heal.

In 1903, Wilbur Wright achieved the first powered flight at Kitty Hawk—a 12-second journey covering 120 feet. But the Wright brothers didn't keep their discovery secret or attempt to maintain a monopoly on flight. Instead, they began teaching others, sharing their knowledge, and equipping a generation of aviators. Within a decade, their students were flying higher, faster, and farther than the Wright brothers ever did. By equipping others rather than hoarding knowledge, they launched not just airplanes but an entire industry that transformed human civilization.

Jesus modeled this principle perfectly in Luke 9. After His disciples had observed His ministry, learned His teachings, and experienced His power, Jesus moved from engagement to equipping. He didn't keep them as perpetual students; He equipped them to become practitioners.

Jesus "gave them power and authority"—not just instructions or information. Many leaders share knowledge without transferring authority, creating dependent followers rather than equipped ministers. True equipping provides both the ability to act and the authority to make decisions.

Jesus' instructions were specific: what to take (nothing extra), where to stay (remain in one house), how to respond to rejection (shake off the dust). Effective equipping doesn't leave people guessing about expectations or boundaries. It provides clear framework within which they can exercise their newfound authority.

Once Jesus equipped the disciples, He sent them out without Him. This is perhaps the hardest aspect of equipping—allowing others to minister without your direct supervision. Many leaders say they want to equip others but struggle to release control when the time comes.

Jesus warned His disciples about rejection: "wherever they do not receive you..." He didn't promise universal success or shield them from difficulty. Instead, He equipped them to handle opposition. Reliable messengers prepare those they equip for both success and setback.

The progression from engagement to equipping is essential. Engagement creates trust and relationship. Observation allows modeling and learning. Equipping transfers knowledge and authority. Practice develops confidence and competence. Release multiplies ministry impact.

In our complex world, equipping others requires more than good intentions. It demands assessment (understanding current abilities and gaps), instruction (providing necessary knowledge), modeling (demonstrating effective ministry), practice (creating safe spaces for trial and error), feedback (offering constructive evaluation), and release (trusting them to minister independently).

When Jesus equipped twelve disciples, they eventually "turned the world upside down." When you equip one person effectively, you don't just double your impact—you potentially multiply it exponentially as they equip others who equip others.

Common obstacles to effective equipping include fear that others won't do things "right," concern about losing significance, impatience with the messy process of development, failure to create systematic equipping processes, and attempting to equip without first engaging.

Living It Out

Reflection Questions:

1. Who has effectively equipped you for ministry, and what made their equipping effective?

2. Who is God calling you to equip, and what's preventing you from doing so?

3. Are you transferring both knowledge and authority, or are you creating dependency?

Weekly Challenge: Identify one person you've been engaging with and take a concrete step toward equipping them. This might mean teaching them a skill, delegating a responsibility with clear authority, or creating an opportunity for them to practice ministry with your support.

Implementation Ideas:

- Create a simple equipping plan for someone you're mentoring.

- Delegate a meaningful responsibility with clear authority to act.

- Share not just what to do but why and how you make decisions.

- Allow someone to shadow you in ministry, then reverse roles.

- Celebrate when those you've equipped surpass your own abilities.

WEEK 39

THE E4 LEADERSHIP MODEL: EMPOWER & ENCOURAGE

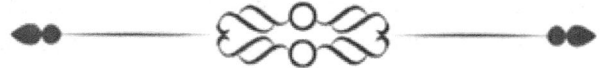

Acts 13:1-3 (ESV) - Now there were in the church at Antioch prophets and teachers, Barnabas, Simeon who was called Niger, Lucius of Cyrene, Manaen a lifelong friend of Herod the tetrarch, and Saul. While they were worshiping the Lord and fasting, the Holy Spirit said, "Set apart for me Barnabas and Saul for the work to which I have called them."

In 1955, Ray Kroc met Mac and Dick McDonald, who had developed an innovative fast-food system in San Bernardino, California. But Kroc saw something the McDonald brothers didn't—the potential for nationwide impact through empowerment. Rather than simply buying their restaurant, Kroc created a franchise system that empowered thousands of entrepreneurs to own and operate their own McDonald's restaurants. He provided the system, training, and support, but empowered individual owners to succeed in their local contexts. Kroc understood that empowering others to succeed would create far greater impact than anything he could accomplish alone.

The church at Antioch demonstrates the culmination of the E4 Leadership Model—empowerment and encouragement working together to release world-changing ministry.

Look at the leadership team at Antioch: Barnabas (a Levite from Cyprus), Simeon called Niger (likely African), Lucius of

Cyrene (North African), Manaen (connected to Herod's court), and Saul (a Pharisee from Tarsus). This diverse team had been engaging together, equipping one another, and now were ready to empower ministry that would impact the world.

"While they were worshiping the Lord and fasting, the Holy Spirit said..." Empowerment isn't just about organizational strategy or leadership development. It requires spiritual discernment to recognize when God is calling someone to a new level of ministry. The church at Antioch created space through worship and fasting to hear the Holy Spirit's direction.

Barnabas and Saul weren't struggling believers who needed something to do. They were key leaders in the Antioch church—prophets and teachers who were vital to the local ministry. True empowerment often means releasing those you'd rather keep, trusting God to fill the gap their departure creates.

"They laid their hands on them and sent them off." This wasn't a quiet, private send-off. The church publicly affirmed Barnabas and Saul's calling, transferring spiritual authority through the laying on of hands. Empowerment includes visible, tangible expressions of trust and commissioning.

The twin dynamics work together. **Empowerment provides** authority to make decisions, resources to accomplish the mission, freedom to develop their own methods, trust to act without constant supervision, and permission to take risks and even fail.

Encouragement provides affirmation of calling and gifting, support during challenging seasons, celebration of victories and progress, comfort in setbacks and failures, and reminders of God's faithfulness.

When Barnabas and Saul were empowered and sent out, they didn't just preach—they replicated the E4 model wherever they went. They engaged new communities with the gospel, equipped new believers with foundational truth, empowered local leaders to lead new churches, and encouraged through return visits and letters.

In our control-oriented culture, true empowerment feels risky. It means allowing others to do things differently than you would, accepting that some ventures will fail, trusting God to work through imperfect people, celebrating when those you've empowered exceed your impact, and finding your joy in their success rather than your own.

Here's what I've learned: empowerment without encouragement often leads to burnout. Notice how Paul's ministry was sustained by encouragement from churches, fellow workers, and the Holy Spirit. Reliable messengers understand that empowerment is not abandonment—it requires ongoing encouragement to sustain momentum.

Common barriers to empowerment and encouragement include fear of being surpassed or replaced, need to maintain control, failure to develop systems for ongoing support, inability to celebrate others' success, and confusion between delegation and empowerment.

Living It Out

Reflection Questions:

1. Who has empowered you for ministry, and how did their encouragement sustain you?

2. Who are you currently equipping that's ready to be empowered for greater ministry?

3. How can you create systems of encouragement that sustain those you've empowered?

Weekly Challenge: Take a specific step to empower someone this week. This might mean giving them authority over a ministry area, publicly affirming their calling, providing resources for their vision, or simply encouraging them in what God has called them to do. Then commit to ongoing encouragement.

Implementation Ideas:

- Identify someone ready to move from equipping to empowerment.

- Create a commissioning moment (formal or informal) for someone you're empowering.

- Write an encouragement note to someone you've previously empowered.

- Release control over something you've been holding too tightly.

- Celebrate publicly when those you've empowered achieve success.

QUARTER 4

LIVING AS RELIABLE MESSENGERS

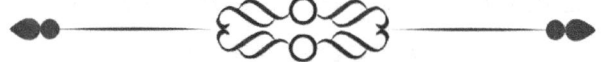

Practical Application and Mission (Weeks 40-52)

Communication and Community

WEEK 40

THE E3 COMMUNICATION: EXPLICIT, EXPLAINABLE, ESSENTIAL

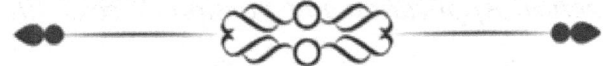

1 Corinthians 14:8-9 (NLT) - And if the bugler doesn't sound a clear call, how will the soldiers know they are being called to battle? It's the same for you. If you speak to people in words they don't understand, how will they know what you are saying? You might as well be talking into empty space.

In 1961, President John F. Kennedy faced a critical communication challenge. The United States was losing the space race to the Soviet Union, Congress was skeptical about funding NASA, and the American public was confused about the nation's space goals. Kennedy could have given a complex technical presentation about orbital mechanics, rocket propulsion, and lunar geology. Instead, he stood before a joint session of Congress and delivered one of history's most effective communication moments: "I believe that this nation should commit itself to achieving the goal, before this decade is out, of landing a man on the moon and returning him safely to the earth." Kennedy later reflected, "I could have spent an hour explaining the technical challenges of lunar exploration, but that would have impressed the scientists while losing everyone else."

Paul understood this same principle when he wrote to the Corinthians: "And if the bugler doesn't sound a clear call, how will the soldiers know they are being called to battle? It's the same for you. If you speak to people in words they don't understand, how will they know what you are saying?"

The E3 communication model—Explicit, Explainable, Essential—provides a framework for communicating God's truth with maximum clarity and impact.

Explicit Communication: Making Your Message Clear

Explicit communication leaves no room for misunderstanding. Your audience knows exactly what you mean without having to guess, interpret, or read between the lines.

When Paul wrote, "Christ died for our sins according to the Scriptures, and that He was buried, and that He rose again the third day according to the Scriptures," he was being explicit about the gospel's essential elements. No confusion, no ambiguity—just clear truth.

Common barriers to explicit communication include assuming others understand concepts that are actually unfamiliar to them, using religious language that has specific meanings in church culture but different meanings in general culture, being indirect about important truths to avoid potential offense, and failing to provide concrete examples of abstract spiritual principles.

Explainable Communication: Keeping Your Message Concise

Explainable communication distills complex truths into understandable concepts without sacrificing accuracy. It respects your audience's time and cognitive capacity while maintaining the integrity of your message.

Jesus was a master of explainable communication. He used

parables to make complex spiritual truths understandable to ordinary people. The parable of the sower, the prodigal son, and the good Samaritan communicate profound truths through simple, memorable stories.

Here's what I've learned: trying to demonstrate your knowledge rather than serve your audience's understanding creates barriers. Including too much information instead of focusing on key points overwhelms people. Using complex theological concepts without adequate explanation alienates listeners. And failing to consider your audience's background and experience level breaks connection.

Essential Communication: Creating Compelling Messages

Essential communication addresses fundamental human needs and concerns. It connects God's truth to the real issues people face, making your message not just understandable but personally compelling.

Old Testament prophets like Isaiah, Jeremiah, and Ezekiel addressed the essential concerns of their day—social justice, spiritual adultery, coming judgment, and future hope. Their messages were compelling because they spoke to the urgent spiritual and social needs of their time.

The most effective communication combines all three elements. For evangelism, your presentation should be explicit about sin and salvation; explainable even to those with no church background; and essential to people's deepest needs. For teaching, your instruction should be explicit about what Scripture says; explainable through illustrations and applications; and essential to how people should live. For encouragement, your words should be explicit about what you see God doing; explainable in terms they can understand; and essential to their current challenges.

Adapting E3 to different contexts requires flexibility. In one-on-one conversations, focus on being explicit about your own experience, explainable through personal examples, and essential to the specific person's circumstances. In small groups, be explicit about biblical principles, explainable through group interaction, and essential to shared interests. In public speaking, be explicit about your main points, explainable through stories, and essential to your audience's common concerns.

E3 Communication requires preparation. It doesn't usually happen spontaneously. You need to understand your audience and their needs, clarify your own thinking about what you want to communicate, find appropriate examples and illustrations, practice your delivery to ensure clarity, and seek feedback to improve your effectiveness.

The goal isn't to impress people with your knowledge or eloquence but to serve them by making God's truth accessible and applicable to their lives. This servant-hearted approach changes both your preparation and your delivery.

Living It Out

Reflection Questions:

1. Which element of E3 communication—explicit, explainable, or essential—is your greatest strength and which needs the most development?

2. How do you adapt your communication style when speaking to different audiences about spiritual matters?

3. What preparation habits would help you communicate God's truth more effectively?

Weekly Challenge: Practice E3 communication this week in at least three different contexts—a conversation with a friend, a teaching or sharing opportunity, and a written communication. Focus on making your message explicit, explainable, and essential.

Implementation Ideas:

- Before important conversations, clarify your main points and how to communicate them clearly.

- Practice explaining spiritual concepts to people who don't share your church background.

- Look for ways to connect biblical truth to practical daily concerns.

- Ask for feedback about the clarity and relevance of your communication.

WEEK 41

GATHER: BUILDING COMMUNITY

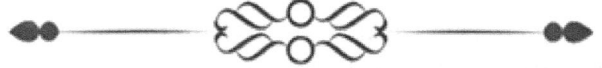

Hebrews 10:24-25 (ESV) - And let us consider how to stir up one another to love and good works, not neglecting to meet together, as is the habit of some, but encouraging one another, and all the more as you see the Day drawing near.

(Story Inspired by True Events) In 1940, London faced its darkest hour as German bombers pounded the city night after night during the Blitz. Many residents fled to the countryside, but those who remained discovered something remarkable in the Underground stations that served as bomb shelters. What began as desperate strangers huddling together for safety evolved into vibrant communities. People who had never spoken to their neighbors before began sharing food, telling stories, singing songs, and caring for each other's children. Winston Churchill later observed, "The Blitz didn't break London's spirit—it revealed it. When people are forced to gather together in the face of danger, they discover they were meant to be together all along."

The GATHER vision calls for reliable messengers to be committed to being together regularly as a faith family, creating safe places of community throughout the week, and staying connected as a leadership team.

The writer of Hebrews doesn't suggest that believers consider gathering together—he commands us not to neglect "to meet together, as is the habit of some." This gathering isn't optional for healthy Christian living.

The Greek word for "assembling" (*episunagoge*) refers to gathering for a specific purpose. Christian gathering isn't just social activity—it's purposeful community designed to accomplish spiritual goals that can't be achieved individually.

Gathering serves multiple essential purposes. There's **mutual encouragement**—"Let us consider one another in order to stir up love and good works." The word "consider" means to observe carefully and think deeply about. Christian community requires intentional attention to one another's spiritual condition and needs.

There's **accountability**—when believers gather regularly, they can observe patterns in each other's lives, celebrate growth, and address concerning changes. This mutual accountability prevents isolation that often leads to spiritual decline.

There's **corporate worship**—while personal worship is important, something powerful happens when believers gather to worship together. Corporate worship creates experiences of God's presence and power that individuals rarely experience alone.

And there's **service coordination**—many forms of ministry and service require coordination and cooperation that happens best when believers gather to plan, pray, and work together.

"Not neglecting to meet together, as is the habit of some" reveals a timeless problem. Even in the first century, some believers were developing a pattern of avoiding church gatherings. The writer suggests this was becoming habitual for some people.

This pattern of avoiding Christian community often develops gradually. First, people attend irregularly due to schedule conflicts or personal preferences. Then they begin finding reasons why gathering isn't necessary for their spiritual growth. Eventually they rationalize their absence as actually being more spiritual than participating in "organized religion." Finally, they lose the community support essential for sustained spiritual growth.

"And so much the more as you see the Day approaching." The writer indicates that as challenges increase—whether personal, cultural, or spiritual—the need for community gathering becomes more urgent, not less.

During seasons of persecution, discouragement, or cultural opposition to Christian values, believers need the encouragement, strength, and perspective that comes from gathering with others who share their commitment to Christ.

The vision to GATHER doesn't happen automatically. It requires deliberate effort to create welcoming environments, foster meaningful relationships, maintain consistent participation, and balance structure with flexibility.

The vision describes "concentric circles" of relationship, recognizing that not all community relationships are identical in depth or function. There's the **inner circle** of close relationships with fellow leaders and mature believers. There's the **middle circle** of regular relationships with others in your church family. And there's the **outer circle** of welcoming relationships with newer believers and visitors.

The purpose of gathering isn't just fellowship for its own sake but growth in "love and good works." Effective Christian community produces character development and increased service to others through challenge and encouragement from other believers, opportunities to practice spiritual gifts, accountability for lifestyle choices, exposure to different perspectives, and corporate prayers that strengthen faith.

Community building requires mutual commitment. Each person must be willing to invest time and energy in building relationships, be vulnerable enough to give and receive encouragement, contribute their gifts to strengthen the community, persist through inevitable conflicts, and prioritize gathering even when other activities compete for attention.

Contemporary culture presents unique obstacles: busy schedules that prioritize achievement over relationships, social media that creates illusion of connection without intimacy, consumer mentality that approaches church as a service provider, mobility that prevents long-term relationship building, and individualism that resists accountability.

Here's the key insight: a strong Christian community prepares believers for more effective mission and service in the world. When believers experience genuine community, they're better equipped to represent Christ to others, work together in ministry, persevere through difficulties, and disciple others.

Living It Out

Reflection Questions:

1. How committed are you to gathering regularly with other believers, and what obstacles interfere with this commitment?

2. In what ways do you contribute to building community rather than just consuming it?

3. How has gathering with other believers strengthened your ability to serve as a reliable messenger?

Weekly Challenge: Take specific action this week to strengthen the gathering aspect of your church community. Whether it's attending more consistently, reaching out to someone who's been absent, or investing more deeply in relationships, contribute to building community.

Implementation Ideas:

- Evaluate your commitment to regular gathering and identify any changes needed.

- Look for ways to encourage others in your church community this week.

- Consider how you can contribute to creating welcoming environments for others.

- If you're not currently part of a consistent gathering community, take steps to find or create one.

WEEK 42

GROW: DISCIPLESHIP MULTIPLICATION

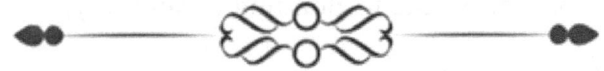

2 Timothy 2:1-2 (AMP) - So you, my son, be strong [constantly strengthened] and empowered in the grace that is [to be found only] in Christ Jesus. The things [the doctrine, the precepts, the admonitions, the sum of my ministry] which you have heard me teach in the presence of many witnesses, entrust [as a treasure] to reliable and faithful men who will also be capable and qualified to teach others.

Florence Nightingale arrived at a British military hospital in Turkey during the Crimean War in 1854. She was horrified to discover that more soldiers were dying from preventable diseases and poor sanitation than from battle wounds. Nightingale didn't just treat individual patients—she developed a revolutionary approach to healthcare that focused on training other nurses. Her method was simple but powerful: she would thoroughly train one experienced nurse, who would then train two others, who would each train two more. Within months, the death rate in military hospitals dropped from 42% to 2%. Nightingale later reflected, "I realized that if I personally treated every wounded soldier, I could help hundreds. But if I trained nurses who trained other nurses, I could help millions."

The GROW vision calls for "steady growth in the amount of people involved in intentional discipling relationships organically and organizationally," recognizing that spiritual growth happens best through intentional investment in developing others who can develop others.

Paul's model in 2 Timothy 2:2 shows four generations: Paul → Timothy → faithful men → others also. This multiplication approach produces exponential growth rather than just linear growth.

If Paul had spent all his time personally discipling individuals, he could have impacted hundreds of people during his lifetime. But by discipling people who discipled others, his influence has continued for nearly 2,000 years and has impacted millions of lives.

The discipleship multiplication process requires several key elements. First, there's **content that can be transmitted**—Paul refers to "the things which you have heard me teach in the presence of many witnesses." Effective discipleship involves specific content—biblical truth, practical wisdom, spiritual disciplines, and ministry skills—that can be passed from one generation to the next.

This content isn't just theological information but practical wisdom about how to live as a follower of Christ, how to study Scripture, how to pray, how to resist temptation, how to serve others, and how to make disciples.

Second, there's **character that can be trusted**—Paul specifies "faithful men," people whose character has been proven reliable over time. Discipleship multiplication requires identifying and investing in people who will faithfully pass on what they receive rather than using it only for personal benefit.

Here's a crucial truth: faithfulness is more important than natural talent. A person with limited abilities but proven character can reproduce discipleship more effectively than someone with great gifts but questionable reliability.

Third, there's **competence that can be developed**—"who will be able to teach others also" indicates that discipleship multiplication requires developing not just personal maturity but ministry competence. People must be equipped not only to follow Christ but to help others follow Christ.

Discipleship multiplication happens both organically and organizationally. **Organic growth** happens through natural relationships where discipleship occurs through friendship, family connections, work relationships, and community involvement. **Organizational growth** happens through intentional programs, classes, small groups, and mentoring relationships designed to facilitate discipleship.

The GROW vision recognizes that everyone should be involved in discipling relationships—both as disciples (learning from others) and as disciplers (investing in others). This creates a culture where everyone is both student and teacher.

This differs from models where only professional ministers or specially trained leaders do discipleship. While leadership is important, multiplication happens best when every believer is actively involved in both learning and teaching.

Common barriers to discipleship multiplication include lack of confidence in ability to disciple others, failure to see discipleship as every believer's responsibility, absence of clear models or systems for discipleship, busyness that crowds out relational investment, and fear of long-term commitment required for effective discipleship.

GROW strategies that overcome these barriers include providing training in basic discipleship methods, creating simple reproducible discipleship tools, celebrating stories of discipleship multiplication, building accountability for discipleship relationships, and demonstrating that discipleship can happen in natural life rhythms.

The beauty of multiplication is its exponential impact. One person discipling one other person each year who then disciples another creates a chain reaction that can impact thousands over time. This is why the GROW vision emphasizes multiplication rather than just addition.

Living It Out

Reflection Questions:

1. Who are you currently learning from as a disciple, and who are you investing in as a discipler?

2. What content (biblical truth, practical wisdom, ministry skills) are you passing on to others?

3. How could you move from informal influence to intentional discipleship relationships?

Weekly Challenge: Take one concrete step this week toward discipleship multiplication. Either initiate a discipling relationship with someone who could benefit from your experience, or ask someone more mature to disciple you in areas where you need growth.

Implementation Ideas:

- Identify specific people you could begin discipling or who could disciple you.

- Develop a simple plan for what you would teach someone you're discipling.

- Look for natural opportunities in your current relationships to add discipleship elements.

- Remember that effective discipleship happens through life-on-life investment, not just formal teaching.

WEEK 43

GO: MISSION MINDED

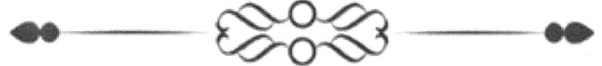

Romans 10:14-15 (AMP) - But how will people call on Him in whom they have not believed? And how will they believe in Him of whom they have not heard? And how will they hear without a preacher (messenger)? And how will they preach unless they are commissioned and sent [for that purpose]? Just as it is written and forever remains written, "How beautiful are the feet of those who bring good news of good things!"

In 1886, a young student named C.T. Studd heard Hudson Taylor speak about the desperate need for missionaries in China. Studd was heir to a substantial fortune and had prospects for a comfortable life in England, but Taylor's message convinced him that comfortable living while people perished without the gospel was incompatible with following Christ. Studd gave away his inheritance, sailed to China as a missionary, and later pioneered missions work in India and Africa. His famous saying, "Some wish to live within the sound of church or chapel bell; I want to run a rescue shop within a yard of hell," exemplifies the GO vision.

The GO vision calls for being more available and useful to our communities (locally and globally) than we ever have before, expanding current offerings and adding new ones locally, and connecting our people with global outreach initiatives.

Paul's logic in Romans 10 is compelling: People cannot call on Christ for salvation unless they believe in Him. They cannot believe unless they hear about Him. They cannot hear unless someone tells them. And people cannot tell them unless they are sent with the message.

This logical sequence makes missions not just a good option for some believers but a necessary activity for the church to fulfill its purpose. Without going, the gospel remains confined to those who already have it while others perish without hope.

Paul quotes Isaiah: "How beautiful are the feet of those who preach the gospel of peace, who bring glad tidings of good things!" This beautiful imagery shows God's perspective on those who carry His message to others.

From a human perspective, missionaries and evangelists often face difficult conditions, dangerous situations, and discouraging responses. But from God's perspective, their willingness to go makes them beautiful because they're participating in His redemptive purposes.

The GO vision emphasizes being "more available and useful to our communities (locally and globally)," recognizing that mission-minded thinking includes both near and far responsibilities.

Your immediate community—neighborhood, workplace, school, city—represents your primary mission field. People around you need to hear the gospel, see Christian love in action, and experience the hope that comes through a relationship with Christ.

But the world beyond your immediate community also needs the gospel. This includes unreached people groups, international communities, and geographic areas where the church has limited presence.

Both dimensions are essential. Local missions without

global vision can become narrow and self-centered. Global missions without local commitment often lack authenticity and practical experience.

The vision calls for "expanding our current offerings and adding new ones locally." This suggests that mission-minded churches are never satisfied with maintaining the status quo—they're always looking for new ways to serve their communities and reach people with the gospel.

This might mean improving existing ministries—better children's programs, more effective small groups, enhanced worship experiences. Or it might mean developing new ministries that address unmet needs—job training programs, addiction recovery groups, senior citizen care.

The vision includes "connecting our people with global outreach initiatives." While not everyone is called to be a full-time missionary, everyone should be connected to global missions in some way—through prayer support, financial support, short-term missions, professional missions, or hosting and welcoming.

Effective mission work recognizes that people have both spiritual needs (forgiveness, salvation, eternal security) and practical needs (food, shelter, healthcare, education). Mission-minded churches address both dimensions, sharing the message of salvation while meeting practical needs, demonstrating God's love through acts of service while explaining the source of that love.

Random acts of service, while valuable, aren't sufficient for an effective mission. The GO vision requires strategic thinking about target populations, effective methods, partnership opportunities, resource allocation, and long-term sustainability.

C.T. Studd's decision to give away his inheritance and go to dangerous places illustrates that mission-minded living often requires sacrifice. While not everyone is called to such dramatic sacrifice, everyone who embraces the GO vision will face costs—financial costs, time costs, comfort costs, and security costs.

While the costs of mission-minded living are real, they're temporary. The results—people coming to Christ, communities being transformed, and God's kingdom advancing—are eternal. This eternal perspective motivates sustained commitment to going even when immediate results are discouraging or costs seem high.

The Great Commission wasn't a suggestion—it was a command. Mission-minded living flows from love for Christ and desire to obey His final instructions to His followers. When you truly understand what Christ has done for you and what He's commanded you to do, going becomes not just an option but a compulsion.

Living It Out

Reflection Questions:

1. How would you honestly assess your current commitment to local and global mission—are you more focused on going or staying comfortable?

2. What specific people groups or geographic areas has God burdened your heart to pray for and potentially serve?

3. How could you expand your current involvement in local community service and global outreach?

Weekly Challenge: Take one concrete step this week toward being more mission-minded. Whether it's starting a conversation with an unbeliever, volunteering in community service, researching global mission opportunities, or increasing your missions giving, move toward greater GO commitment.

Implementation Ideas:

- Research specific unreached people groups and begin praying for them regularly.

- Look for practical ways to serve needs in your local community.

- Consider how your career skills could be used in cross-cultural ministry contexts.

- Connect with missionaries or mission organizations to learn about partnership opportunities.

The T4 Stewardship Model

WEEK 44

T4: INVESTING TIME

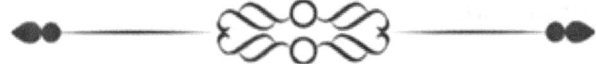

Ephesians 5:15-16 (ESV) - Look carefully then how you walk, not as unwise but as wise, making the best use of the time, because the days are evil.

Benjamin Franklin once wrote, "Remember that time is money," but for reliable messengers, the equation is different: time is opportunity for kingdom impact. Every moment represents potential for advancing God's purposes or missed opportunity for eternal significance.

The first element of T4 stewardship—Time—calls reliable messengers to invest their most precious resource wisely in partnership with the local church for maximum kingdom impact.

Time is unique among all resources because it's the only one that's distributed equally. Rich and poor, educated and uneducated, healthy and sick—everyone receives exactly 24 hours each day. How you invest this irreplaceable resource reveals your true priorities and determines your ultimate legacy.

Paul's instruction to "Look carefully then how you walk, not as unwise but as wise," connects time management to spiritual wisdom. Wise time investment goes beyond efficiency and productivity to consider eternal significance and kingdom purposes.

Characteristics of wise time investment include prioritizing activities with eternal significance over temporal value, balancing urgent demands with important long-term objectives, including adequate time for spiritual disciplines, considering the needs of others, and seeking God's guidance about priorities.

The phrase "making the best use of time" means redeeming the time, buying up or buying back time, like purchasing something valuable from a marketplace. Paul suggests that time can be lost through poor choices but can also be reclaimed through wise decisions.

This redemption metaphor indicates that time isn't just spent—it's invested with expectation of return. Reliable messengers approach time management as stewardship, accountable to God for how they use the hours He's entrusted to them.

The T4 framework specifically emphasizes "investing your time in kingdom work through partnering with the local church." This isn't just general religious activity but strategic partnership with the local body of believers for maximum kingdom impact.

Why partnership with the local church? There's multiplication of impact—individual efforts can't match coordinated community action. There's mutual accountability for consistent service. There's complementary gifts that make your time more effective. There's sustainable systems that continue beyond individual participation. And, there's a global connection that amplifies local time investment.

Here's what I've discovered: wise time investment requires saying no to good things in order to say yes to God things. In a culture with unlimited opportunities for involvement, careful discernment is essential about which activities deserve your limited hours.

Criteria for time investment decisions include asking: Does this align with my spiritual gifts and calling? Will this contribute to advancing God's kingdom? Can I participate without neglecting higher priorities? Does this provide opportunities for spiritual growth? Is this something God is specifically leading me to do?

Effective time investment balances giving to others with receiving from God. All service without adequate spiritual intake leads to burnout; all intake without service leads to spiritual stagnation. You need both service time (using your time to meet others' needs) and development time (investing time in activities that increase your spiritual maturity).

Unlike money, which can be saved and accumulated, time must be spent as it's received. The question isn't whether you'll spend your time but how you'll invest it and what legacy those investments will create.

Paul's warning that "the days are evil" reminds us that we live in a fallen world where time is limited and opposition to God's purposes is real. This urgency should motivate strategic time investment rather than a casual approach to how we spend our days.

Common time wasters that hinder kingdom investment include entertainment that provides temporary pleasure but no lasting value, worry about circumstances beyond your control, perfectionism that prevents completion, people-pleasing that leads to commitments based on pressure rather than calling, and procrastination that delays important tasks until they become urgent crises.

Like financial investments, time investments should be regularly reviewed to ensure they're producing desired results and remain aligned with current priorities and calling. When you invest time wisely in kingdom work, especially through partnership with the local church, your influence extends beyond the hours you personally contribute.

Living It Out

Reflection Questions:

1. How would you honestly assess your current time investment—what percentage goes toward kingdom work versus personal pursuits?

2. What activities are you currently involved in that may not be the best use of your time for kingdom purposes?

3. How could you better coordinate your time investment with your local church's mission and ministries?

Weekly Challenge: Conduct a time audit this week, tracking how you actually spend your hours for several days. Then evaluate whether your time investment aligns with your stated priorities and calling as a reliable messenger.

Implementation Ideas:

- Create a weekly schedule that prioritizes kingdom work while maintaining balance.

- Identify time wasters that you can eliminate to create space for more meaningful investment.

- Look for specific ways to partner with your local church in ministry that matches your gifts.

- Develop systems for regularly evaluating and adjusting your time investments.

WEEK 45

T4: INVESTING TALENT

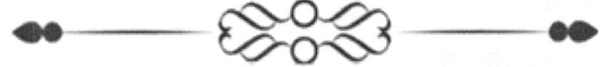

1 Peter 4:10-11 (NLT) - God has given each of you a gift from his great variety of spiritual gifts. Use them well to serve one another. Do you have the gift of speaking? Then speak as though God himself were speaking through you. Do you have the gift of helping others? Do it with all the strength and energy that God supplies.

In 1905, a young Albert Einstein was working as a patent clerk in Switzerland, spending his days evaluating other people's inventions. Many would have considered this a waste of his remarkable intellectual gifts. But Einstein understood something profound: he could use even a mundane job as a platform for expressing his God-given talents. During lunch breaks and after work, he developed the theories that would revolutionize physics and change our understanding of the universe.

The second element of T4 stewardship—Talent—focuses on investing our unique abilities "through the opportunities for service in and through the local church" for God's glory and others' benefit.

Peter's instruction assumes that "God has given each of you a gift"—not some people, not just specially talented individuals, but everyone. The Greek word for gift (*charisma*) emphasizes that these abilities are expressions of God's grace, given not because we deserve them but because God chooses to work through us.

This universal giftedness means that no believer can legitimately claim to have nothing to contribute. While gifts vary in type and prominence, everyone has received abilities that God intends to use for blessing others.

The purpose of gifts is clear: "minister it to one another, as good stewards of the manifold grace of God." Gifts aren't given primarily for personal benefit, career advancement, or social recognition—they're given for service to others.

This service orientation transforms how you view your abilities. Instead of asking "How can I use my talents to get ahead?" you ask "How can I use my talents to serve others and advance God's kingdom?"

Peter describes believers as "stewards" of God's grace. A steward manages someone else's property and is accountable for how those resources are used. Your talents ultimately belong to God, and you're responsible for investing them wisely according to His purposes.

This stewardship perspective eliminates both pride (your gifts are from God) and false humility (refusing to use gifts God has given). You're neither the owner of your abilities nor free to neglect them—you're a trusted manager accountable for wise investment.

The T4 framework emphasizes investing talents "through the opportunities for service in and through the local church." This doesn't mean all ministry must happen within church walls, but it does mean coordinating your service with the local body of believers for maximum effectiveness.

Why coordinate your talents through the local church? Because your abilities combined with others' create greater impact. Because mature leadership helps ensure quality and biblical alignment. Because you're building something that lasts beyond yourself. Because you need encouragement when service gets hard. And because the church provides training to help you serve more effectively.

Before you can invest your talents wisely, you need to understand what they are. There are **spiritual gifts**—supernatural abilities given by the Holy Spirit for ministry. There are **natural talents**—abilities you were born with or developed early. And there are **learned skills**—competencies developed through education, training, and experience.

Effective talent investment often combines multiple types of abilities. A reliable messenger might use professional skills (learned through career development), natural communication ability, and the spiritual gift of teaching to serve effectively in Christian education ministry.

While willingness to serve is admirable, wise stewardship requires matching your service with your abilities for maximum impact. The church benefits more when people serve in areas where their gifts can be most effective.

Questions for talent assessment: What activities energize me and produce good results? What do mature believers say they see as my strengths? Where have I seen God bless my service beyond my natural ability? What needs in my church match my abilities and passions? Where can I serve in ways that help develop others' gifts as well?

Peter's instruction to serve "with the ability which God supplies" indicates that talent investment should be characterized by both faithful effort and excellence in execution. This balance prevents both sloppiness (justifying poor service by claiming good intentions) and perfectionism (refusing to serve until you feel completely qualified).

Like the other T4 elements, talent investment is most effective when it includes reproduction—using your gifts to help others discover and develop their gifts through mentoring, training, creating opportunities, and encouragement.

Using your gifts in service to others often costs time, energy, and resources you could have used for personal benefit. But it produces deep satisfaction that comes from fulfilling your God-given purpose. This satisfaction is qualitatively different from the temporary pleasure that comes from self-centered use of talents.

Your gifts and abilities will change over time—some may increase, others may decrease, and you may discover new ones. But the call to invest them in service continues throughout life, adapting to changing circumstances and opportunities.

Living It Out

Reflection Questions:

1. How clearly have you identified your spiritual gifts, natural talents, and learned skills?

2. Are you currently investing your abilities primarily for personal benefit or for service to others through the church?

3. What prevents you from more fully investing your talents in kingdom work?

Weekly Challenge: Take one specific step this week toward better investment of your talents through service opportunities in and through your local church. Whether it's volunteering for a ministry that matches your gifts, offering to help with a project that needs your skills, or simply asking leadership how you can serve more effectively.

Implementation Ideas:

- Complete a spiritual gifts assessment or ask mature believers to help you identify your gifts.

- Look for service opportunities in your church that match your abilities and interests.

- Consider how your professional skills could be used for ministry purposes.

- Find ways to help others discover and develop their gifts through your service.

WEEK 46

T4: INVESTING TREASURE

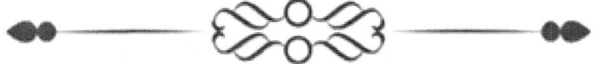

2 Corinthians 9:6-8 (AMP) - Now [remember] this: he who sows sparingly will also reap sparingly, and he who sows generously [that blessings may come to others] will also reap generously [and be blessed]. Let each one give [thoughtfully and with purpose] just as he has decided in his heart, not grudgingly or under compulsion, for God loves a cheerful giver [and delights in the one whose heart is in his gift].

In 1915, John D. Rockefeller Sr. made a decision that would define his legacy. Despite being one of the wealthiest men in history, he chose to give away most of his fortune during his lifetime, ultimately donating over $540 million (equivalent to billions today) to charitable causes. Rockefeller understood something profound: "I believe that every right implies a responsibility; every opportunity, an obligation; every possession, a duty."

The third element of T4 stewardship—Treasure—focuses on investing financial resources "in the ministry of the local church as generous and faithful givers" for kingdom impact.

"He who sows sparingly will also reap sparingly, and he who sows generously will also reap generously." Paul uses agricultural imagery to show that giving, like farming, follows predictable principles. The harvest corresponds to the planting—both in quantity and quality.

This principle applies to both spiritual and material dimensions. Generous giving often results in material blessings, but it always produces spiritual benefits—joy, purpose, trust in God, freedom from materialism, and participation in God's eternal work.

"Let each one give just as he has decided in his heart, not grudgingly or under compulsion, for God loves a cheerful giver." The word "cheerful" (*hilaros*) is where we get "hilarious"—God loves givers who find joy in their generosity rather than viewing it as burdensome obligation.

This joy comes from understanding that giving is opportunity to participate in God's work, not just financial obligation. When you see your treasure as a tool for advancing God's kingdom rather than just personal security, giving becomes exciting rather than stressful.

"And God is able to make all grace come in abundance to you, so that you may always have complete sufficiency in everything." Paul promises that God provides not just enough for personal needs but abundance that enables generous giving.

This doesn't guarantee wealth or promise that generous givers will never face financial challenges. It does promise that God provides what's needed to live and give according to His calling on your life.

While Paul emphasizes voluntary giving, other Scripture passages indicate that treasure investment should be planned rather than sporadic. The principle of tithing provides a starting point, but mature believers often give much more as their resources and understanding increase.

Biblical guidelines for treasure investment include giving firstfruits (before spending on other things), giving proportionally (based on income), giving as planned (budgeting for giving), giving progressively (increasing percentage as income increases), and giving sacrificially (enough that it requires trust in God).

Jesus warned about storing up treasures on earth where they can be destroyed or stolen, and encouraged storing treasures in heaven where they're eternally secure. Reliable messengers view their giving as an investment strategy for eternal returns.

Categories of eternal treasure investment include local church ministry, global missions, discipleship and training, community service, and emergency assistance. Each category contributes to advancing God's kingdom in different ways.

The T4 framework specifically emphasizes giving "in the ministry of the local church" because coordinated giving through the church body creates greater impact than individual giving alone. Advantages include multiplication of resources, oversight for wise use, sustainability of ongoing programs, tax benefits that increase giving capacity, and strategic planning for long-term effectiveness.

Not all charitable giving produces equal kingdom impact. Reliable messengers should evaluate giving opportunities based on their alignment with biblical priorities and effectiveness in accomplishing stated goals.

Here's what I've learned: effective treasure investment usually includes both consistent, budgeted giving to support ongoing ministry and occasional special gifts to support capital projects, emergency needs, or new ministry opportunities.

In a consumer culture that constantly encourages spending, generous giving often requires deliberate lifestyle choices that prioritize eternal values over immediate gratification. Common adjustments include choosing less expensive housing, driving older vehicles longer, eating out less frequently, choosing less expensive entertainment, and delaying purchases.

These adjustments aren't burdensome deprivation but strategic choices that align spending with eternal priorities.

Here's what might surprise you: generous givers often have more financial peace than those who hoard wealth. When you invest your money in God's kingdom instead of stockpiling it for security, you discover a different kind of peace—the kind that comes from trusting God's provision rather than your bank account.

Living It Out

Reflection Questions:

1. What percentage of your income are you currently investing in God's kingdom through your local church and other ministry?

2. What fears or attachments to money prevent you from being more generous in your treasure investment?

3. How could you adjust your lifestyle to free additional resources for kingdom investment?

Weekly Challenge: Take one specific step this week toward more faithful treasure investment. Whether it's increasing your regular giving percentage, making a special gift to support a ministry need, or adjusting your budget to allow for greater generosity, move toward greater faithfulness in this area.

Implementation Ideas:

- Create a giving budget that treats generosity as a priority rather than an afterthought.

- Research specific ministries your church supports to understand how your giving creates kingdom impact.

- Consider automatic giving systems that ensure consistent treasure investment.

- Look for ways to involve your family in giving decisions to teach biblical stewardship principles.

WEEK 47

T4: INVESTING TESTIMONY

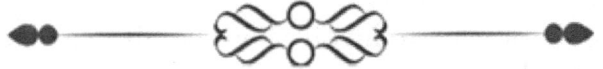

Acts 1:6-8 (ESV) - So when they had come together, they asked him, "Lord, will you at this time restore the kingdom to Israel?" He said to them, "It is not for you to know times or seasons that the Father has fixed by his own authority. But you will receive power when the Holy Spirit has come upon you, and you will be my witnesses..."

On a cold February morning in 1960, four African American college freshmen sat down at a whites-only lunch counter in Greensboro, North Carolina. They weren't just seeking service—they were investing their testimony in the cause of justice. Their quiet dignity in the face of hostility, their commitment to nonviolence despite provocation, and their persistence despite arrest created a testimony that sparked a nationwide movement. Within months, similar sit-ins occurred in over 100 cities.

The fourth element of T4 stewardship—Testimony—focuses on investing our personal stories and witness "for the advancement of the Gospel through the church, to the nations, for the Kingdom."

Jesus' promise in Acts 1:8—"You shall be witnesses to Me"—applies to every follower, not just those with dramatic conversion stories or spectacular spiritual experiences. The word "witnesses" (*martys*) refers to people who testify about what they've seen and experienced personally.

Your testimony is the unique story of God's work in your life, and it's one of your most powerful tools as a reliable messenger. Unlike theological arguments that can be debated or disputed, your personal testimony carries the weight of lived experience that's difficult to refute.

Your testimony includes how you came to faith in Christ, what God has done in your life, how faith affects your daily life, and what you've learned about God's character. Each element provides different opportunities for connection with others.

The T4 framework emphasizes investing testimony "for the advancement of the Gospel." This means your testimony should ultimately point people toward Jesus Christ and His saving work rather than just inspiring general religious sentiment.

Elements of Gospel-advancing testimony include being clear about your need for salvation, specific about Christ's work, personal about transformation, and inviting about response. Each element helps others understand not just your story but how they can experience the same salvation and transformation.

Your testimony should be coordinated "through the church, to the nations, for the Kingdom." **Through the church** provides training, accountability, and support systems that make your testimony more credible and effective. **To the nations** means your testimony should contribute to global evangelization. **For the Kingdom** means the ultimate purpose is advancing God's Kingdom.

While testimony should be authentic and personal rather than scripted, it's helpful to think through how to share your story clearly and compellingly. Elements of prepared testimony include a brief summary for casual conversations, a detailed version for formal sharing, specific applications for different audiences, supporting Scripture that relates to your experience, and response guidance for those interested in learning more.

Most effective testimony investment happens through natural relationships and conversations. Natural testimony opportunities arise in crisis situations, success celebrations, holidays and life transitions, community service, and professional relationships. Each provides different openings for spiritual conversations.

Your verbal testimony is validated or undermined by your lifestyle testimony. People are more likely to be influenced by what you say about God when it's consistent with how you live. Lifestyle testimony elements include integrity, love, hope, forgiveness, and generosity.

Sharing your faith story often involves risk—potential rejection, misunderstanding, or conflict with people whose values differ from yours. Common fears include fear of rejection, inadequacy, hypocrisy, and failure. These fears are natural but shouldn't prevent testimony investment.

While you should be ready to share your testimony whenever opportunities arise, strategic thinking can make your testimony investment more effective. Strategic considerations include audience awareness, timing sensitivity, cultural competence, partnership opportunities, and follow-up planning.

Like other forms of T4 stewardship, testimony investment is most effective when it includes helping others learn to share their own testimonies effectively through testimony training, witnessing partnerships, testimony documentation, and encouragement and accountability.

Unlike financial investments that eventually lose value or time investments that end when you die, testimony investment has eternal consequences. Every person who comes to faith through your witness becomes part of your eternal legacy, and their testimony investment may influence countless others through subsequent generations.

Living It Out

Reflection Questions:

1. How prepared are you to share your testimony clearly and compellingly in different situations?

2. What fears or obstacles prevent you from investing your testimony more boldly for Gospel advancement?

3. How could you better coordinate your testimony investment with your local church's evangelistic efforts?

Weekly Challenge: Look for at least one opportunity this week to invest your testimony in advancing the Gospel. Whether it's sharing your faith story with a friend, writing about your spiritual experience, or simply living in ways that create curiosity about your faith, take a step toward bolder testimony investment.

Implementation Ideas:

- Write out your testimony in both brief and detailed versions and practice sharing it naturally.

- Ask God to show you people in your sphere of influence who need to hear your testimony.

- Look for ways to participate in your church's evangelistic activities and training opportunities.

- Consider how your testimony could be shared through social media, writing, or other platforms.

Living It Out

WEEK 48

SERVANT LEADERSHIP IN ACTION

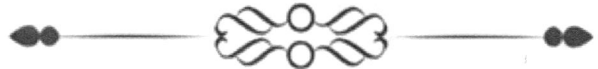

Mark 10:42-45 (ESV) - And Jesus called them to him and said to them, "You know that those who are considered rulers of the Gentiles lord it over them, and their great ones exercise authority over them. But it shall not be so among you. But whoever would be great among you must be your servant...

In 1982, Johnson & Johnson faced a crisis that could have destroyed the company. Seven people in Chicago died after taking Tylenol capsules that had been laced with cyanide. CEO James Burke had a choice: he could minimize the company's responsibility to protect profits, or he could put customer safety above everything else. Burke immediately ordered a nationwide recall of all Tylenol products—31 million bottles worth over $100 million—even though the tampering had occurred after the products left their facilities. Burke's decision to serve customers' interests rather than shareholders' short-term profits cost the company enormous immediate losses but ultimately saved the brand. Years later, Burke reflected, "The customer must come first, the employee second, and the shareholder third."

Jesus' teaching on servant leadership represents one of the most counter-cultural concepts in Scripture, directly opposing the world's understanding of leadership, power, and success.

"You know that those who are considered rulers over the Gentiles lord it over them, and their great ones exercise authority over them." Jesus describes the typical pattern of earthly leadership—using position and power to gain personal benefit, demanding service from others, and maintaining authority through control and dominance.

"But it shall not be so among you. But whoever would be great among you must be your servant, and whoever would be first among you must be slave of all." Jesus establishes a completely different paradigm where greatness is measured by service rather than status, and leadership is defined by what you give rather than what you receive.

The word "servant" (*diakonos*) refers to someone who serves at table, meeting others' needs before their own. The word "slave" (*doulos*) goes even further, describing someone who has no rights of their own but exists entirely for their master's benefit.

"For even the Son of Man came not to be served but to serve, and to give his life as a ransom for many." Jesus doesn't just teach servant leadership—He demonstrates it through His incarnation, ministry, and sacrificial death.

Servant leadership requires several key characteristics. There's **leading through influence rather than authority**—while servant leaders may hold positions of authority, they lead primarily through moral influence, earned respect, and demonstrated competence rather than through demands for obedience.

There's **focusing on others' development**—servant leaders measure success by how well they develop other people rather than by their own achievements, recognition, or accumulation of power and resources.

There's **meeting needs rather than creating dependency**—true servant leadership empowers others to succeed rather than keeping them dependent on the leader's continued involvement. The goal is to work yourself out of a job by developing others who can do what you do.

And there's **sacrificing for others' benefit**—servant leadership often involves personal sacrifice—time, comfort, recognition, resources, or opportunities—for the benefit of those you serve.

Servant leadership challenges common misconceptions. It's not weakness but strength—it requires great strength to serve others when you have the power to demand service from them. It's not about popularity but effectiveness—sometimes servant leaders must make unpopular decisions or give difficult feedback. And while servant leaders treat others with dignity and respect, they don't abdicate their leadership responsibility.

Servant leadership applies in different contexts—family leadership (serving families' best interests), church leadership (serving the congregation's spiritual growth), business leadership (serving employees and customers), and community leadership (serving the common good).

The natural human tendency is to use any power or position for personal advantage. Servant leadership goes against this tendency and requires spiritual motivation that comes from understanding Christ's example and calling.

While self-serving leadership may produce short-term results through fear, manipulation, or coercion, servant leadership creates lasting change through inspiration, development, and reproduction. People who have been served well by leaders often become servant leaders themselves.

Choosing to serve rather than be served often involves

immediate costs—less recognition, more work, fewer privileges, and greater responsibility for others' welfare. But these costs are far outweighed by the rewards—deeper relationships, lasting impact, spiritual satisfaction, and ultimately greater influence than self-serving leaders ever achieve.

Living It Out

Reflection Questions:

1. In what areas of your life do you have leadership influence, and how could you serve others better in those roles?

2. What motivations drive your leadership—desire to serve others or desire for personal benefit?

3. How has Christ's servant leadership toward you motivated your own service to others?

Weekly Challenge: Identify one specific way you can practice servant leadership this week. Look for opportunities to use whatever influence or authority you have to serve others' best interests rather than your own.

Implementation Ideas:

- Study Jesus' examples of servant leadership throughout the Gospels.

- Ask people you lead how you could serve them better and help them succeed.

- Look for ways to develop others' abilities rather than just benefiting from their service.

- Practice making decisions based on others' welfare rather than your own convenience.

WEEK 49

LIVING WITH GRATITUDE

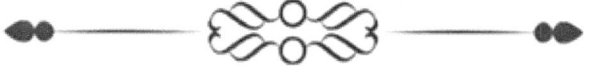

1 Thessalonians 5:16-18 (ESV) - Rejoice always, pray without ceasing, give thanks in all circumstances; for this is the will of God in Christ Jesus for you.

In 1968, Robert F. Kennedy was campaigning for president when he received devastating news: Martin Luther King Jr. had been assassinated. Kennedy was scheduled to speak that evening in Indianapolis, in the heart of an African American neighborhood that hadn't yet heard the news. Police advised him to cancel, fearing riots. Instead, Kennedy stood on a flatbed truck and delivered what many consider one of the greatest speeches in American history. He shared the tragic news, then spoke of his own brother's assassination, and concluded with words of hope rather than hatred. While riots erupted in over 100 cities that night, Indianapolis remained peaceful. Years later, community leaders said it was Kennedy's authentic gratitude for Dr. King's life and vision—expressed even in the midst of devastating loss—that helped heal rather than inflame their hearts.

Living with gratitude represents the heart attitude that sustains all other aspects of being a reliable messenger. It's the foundation that enables you to serve joyfully, give generously, and persist faithfully regardless of circumstances.

"Rejoice always, pray without ceasing, in everything give thanks." Paul's trilogy of commands creates a lifestyle of spiritual awareness and positive response to God's presence in all circumstances.

Rejoice always: The word "rejoice" means to be cheerful, glad, or full of joy. This isn't superficial happiness dependent on circumstances but deep-seated joy rooted in relationship with God and confidence in His purposes.

Pray without ceasing: Constant prayer maintains awareness of God's presence and creates ongoing conversation with Him throughout daily activities. This prayer-saturated life enables gratitude because you're consistently aware of God's involvement in your circumstances.

Give thanks in everything: The phrase "in everything" doesn't mean "for everything" but "in the midst of everything." While we may not be thankful for suffering, injustice, or loss, we can find reasons for gratitude even during difficult situations.

"For this is the will of God in Christ Jesus for you." Paul doesn't present gratitude as a helpful suggestion but as divine expectation. God's will includes His desire that His people live with grateful hearts regardless of external circumstances.

This means gratitude isn't optional for reliable messengers—it's obedience. When you choose ingratitude, complaint, or bitterness, you're choosing to live outside God's will for your life.

Living with gratitude changes how you interpret events, relationships, and opportunities. Instead of focusing on what's wrong, missing, or difficult, gratitude trains you to notice what's right, present, and beneficial.

There's gratitude about the past (recognizing God's faithfulness through previous experiences), gratitude in the present (noticing daily blessings that are easy to overlook), and gratitude for the future (trusting God's promises about what He will do).

People are naturally drawn to grateful individuals because gratitude creates attractive qualities—contentment, joy, peace, and a positive perspective that stands out in a culture characterized by complaint and dissatisfaction.

Your gratitude becomes part of your testimony as a reliable messenger. When people see you maintaining thankfulness during difficult circumstances, they become curious about the source of your hope and strength.

Like Kennedy's grateful remembrance of Dr. King inspiring peace rather than violence, your thankful attitude can influence others to recognize blessings they've been overlooking and find hope in situations that seem hopeless.

Gratitude counteracts common spiritual dangers. It prevents pride by recognizing that achievements come from God rather than your own merit. It reduces materialism by creating contentment with what you have. It prevents bitterness by focusing on God's goodness rather than disappointments. And it builds faith by rehearsing evidence of God's care and provision.

General gratitude is good, but specific gratitude is better. Instead of generic "thank you for everything" prayers, identify particular blessings, provisions, opportunities, and evidence of God's work in your life.

While ultimate gratitude belongs to God, grateful living includes appreciating the people through whom God works—family members, friends, pastors, teachers, coworkers, and even strangers who contribute to your welfare.

While some people seem naturally grateful, gratitude is

primarily a choice and habit that can be developed through intentional practice. Daily gratitude lists, gratitude prayers, appreciation exercises, perspective comparisons, and memory rehearsal all help cultivate a grateful heart.

Here's what I've discovered: when you maintain focus on gratitude, you can find reasons for hope even during disappointing seasons. Like Paul and Silas singing hymns in prison, grateful people can maintain joy and effectiveness even in adverse circumstances.

People who are grateful for small blessings and opportunities are typically ready to handle larger ones responsibly. God often entrusts greater ministry opportunities to people who have demonstrated faithfulness and gratitude in smaller circumstances.

The most authentic worship comes from hearts that have genuinely experienced God's goodness and are responding with thanksgiving. This authentic worship is contagious and draws others toward God.

Living It Out

Reflection Questions:

1. How would others describe your typical attitude— grateful and positive, or complaining and negative?

2. What specific aspects of God's goodness in your life do you need to acknowledge more regularly?

3. How does living with gratitude affect your effectiveness as a reliable messenger?

Weekly Challenge: Practice specific gratitude this week by keeping a daily list of at least three things you're thankful for, expressing appreciation to at least one person each day, and looking for opportunities to share God's goodness with others.

Implementation Ideas:

- Start and end each day by listing specific reasons for gratitude.

- Write thank-you notes to people who have influenced your life positively.

- Share testimonies about God's goodness with other believers to encourage their faith.

- Look for opportunities to express gratitude even during challenging circumstances.

WEEK 50

PARTNERS IN THE MISSION

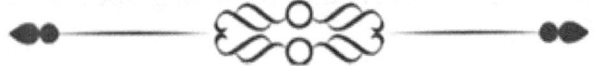

Philippians 1:3-6 (AMP) - I thank my God in every remembrance of you, always offering every prayer of mine with joy [and with specific requests] for all of you, [thanking God] for your participation and partnership [both your comforting fellowship and gracious contributions] in [advancing] the good news...

(Teaching Illustration) On a sweltering August day in 1960, a young missionary doctor named David Thompson arrived in Cameroon, West Africa, carrying two suitcases and a heart full of vision for building a hospital in one of the world's most challenging environments. Forty years later, that vision had become the Banso Baptist Hospital, serving hundreds of thousands of patients and training countless local healthcare workers. But Thompson would be the first to tell you that this mission was never accomplished alone. It required partners— local believers who provided cultural wisdom, supporting churches that provided financial resources, medical colleagues who provided expertise, and family members who provided emotional support.

Partnership in mission represents one of the most essential and often overlooked aspects of effective ministry. The lone ranger approach to Christian service may seem heroic, but it's neither biblical nor sustainable.

"I thank my God in every remembrance of you, always offering every prayer of mine with joy for all of you, for your participation and partnership in the good news from the first day until now." Paul's joy came not from personal achievements but from shared partnership with the Philippians in advancing the gospel.

The word "fellowship" (*koinonia*) means partnership, sharing, or participation together in a common enterprise. This wasn't just friendly cooperation but deep spiritual unity around shared mission and mutual commitment to each other's success.

Paul's confidence that God would complete the work He began wasn't based on his own abilities or the Philippians' natural strengths but on God's faithfulness working through their partnership. Individual effort, no matter how talented or dedicated, has limitations. But partnership multiplies resources, shares burdens, provides accountability, and creates sustainability.

Effective mission partnership requires several key elements. **Shared vision**—partners must be united around common understanding of what they're trying to accomplish and why it matters. **Mutual commitment**—true partnership involves bidirectional commitment where each party invests in the others' success. **Complementary contributions**—effective partnerships combine different strengths, resources, and abilities. **Sustained involvement**—Paul celebrates the Philippians' partnership "from the first day until now," indicating long-term commitment.

Mission partnership operates on multiple levels. **Local partnership** involves working together with other members of your local church. **Regional partnership** involves collaborating with other churches and Christian organizations in your area. **Global partnership** involves supporting and participating in international missions and worldwide church planting efforts.

Healthy mission partnership is mutually beneficial rather

than one-directional charity. While partners contribute different resources and abilities, each should receive value from the relationship. You might contribute financial resources, prayer support, volunteer service, professional skills, relational networks, or leadership abilities. You might receive spiritual growth, broader perspective, accountability and encouragement, training and development, joy and satisfaction, or relationships with people who share your values.

Effective partnership depends on regular, honest communication about needs, resources, successes, failures, and changing circumstances. This communication should include clear agreements, regular updates, honest feedback, forward-looking discussions, and personal sharing that builds relationships.

Partners should hold each other accountable for faithful stewardship of resources, effective ministry methods, spiritual integrity, and progress toward shared goals. This accountability isn't harsh judgment but loving concern for each other's success and faithfulness.

When reliable messengers work together in partnership, their combined influence far exceeds what they could accomplish individually. This multiplication happens through resource pooling, skill coordination, network expansion, credibility enhancement, and sustainability creation.

One person's achievements rarely survive them. But when people partner together, they build something that outlasts any individual—the knowledge gets passed down, the systems keep working, and new leaders step up to continue the mission long after the founders are gone.

The Trinity models perfect partnership—three distinct persons united in perfect relationship for common purposes. When believers work together in mission partnership, they reflect God's relational nature and demonstrate the unity that draws people to faith.

Living It Out

Reflection Questions:

1. Who are your current partners in mission, and how effectively are you working together to advance the gospel?

2. What unique contributions do you bring to mission partnerships, and what do you need from others to be more effective?

3. How could you be a better partner in your local church's mission and in broader ministry efforts?

Weekly Challenge: Take one specific step this week to strengthen your partnership in mission. Whether it's communicating more effectively with current partners, offering to support someone else's ministry efforts, or exploring new partnership opportunities, invest in collaborative ministry.

Implementation Ideas:

- Identify the mission partnerships you're currently involved in and evaluate their effectiveness.

- Look for ways to contribute more meaningfully to your local church's ministry efforts.

- Research mission organizations or initiatives that could benefit from your partnership.

- Practice the partnership qualities of clear communication, mutual commitment, and shared vision.

WEEK 51

THE EXTRAORDINARY LIFE

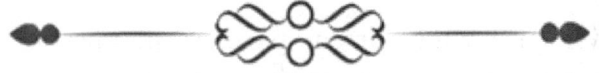

John 10:7-11 (ESV) - So Jesus again said to them, "Truly, truly, I say to you, I am the door of the sheep... I came that they may have life and have it abundantly. I am the good shepherd. The good shepherd lays down his life for the sheep."

In 1952, Elisabeth Elliot faced an unthinkable decision. Her husband Jim had been killed by the Auca Indians in Ecuador while attempting to share the gospel with them. She could have returned to the safety of America, bitter and broken. Instead, she made an extraordinary choice: she learned the Auca language and returned to live among the very people who had killed her husband, eventually seeing many of them come to faith in Christ. Years later, she reflected, "The secret is Christ in me, not me in a different set of circumstances."

The extraordinary life Jesus offers represents the culmination of everything we've learned about being reliable messengers. It's the life that flows from encounter, experience, exchange, endeavor, and encouragement—a life so different from ordinary existence that it demonstrates God's transforming power to everyone who observes it.

"The thief does not come except to steal, and to kill, and to destroy. I have come that they may have life, and that they may have it more abundantly." Jesus contrasts two completely different approaches to life—one that diminishes and destroys, another that enriches and fulfills.

The thief's methods include stealing (taking away joy, peace, purpose), killing (destroying life, dreams, potential), and destroying (ruining what was good, beautiful, and meaningful).

Jesus' method is to give life—not just existence but meaningful, purposeful, joyful life—and give abundance (life that overflows with satisfaction, impact, and eternal significance).

The word "abundantly" (*perissos*) means exceedingly, beyond measure, or more than enough. This doesn't necessarily mean longer life, more possessions, or easier circumstances. It means life of such quality and meaning that it exceeds ordinary human experience.

This abundance includes purpose that transcends circumstances, joy that survives difficulties, peace that surpasses understanding, love that overcomes barriers, and hope that endures setbacks.

Like Elisabeth Elliot choosing to serve those who had wronged her, the extraordinary life involves choices that seem unusual or even foolish from worldly perspective but make perfect sense from kingdom perspective.

Extraordinary choices include forgiveness instead of revenge, service instead of success, generosity instead of accumulation, humility instead of pride, and faith instead of fear.

Jesus doesn't offer abundant life only to naturally gifted, wealthy, or specially privileged individuals. Throughout His ministry, He demonstrated that ordinary people—fishermen, tax collectors, women, children, outcasts—could experience extraordinary transformation and impact.

"I am the good shepherd. The good shepherd lays down his

life for the sheep." Similarly, experiencing abundant life requires laying down lesser pursuits to embrace greater ones. This laying down isn't self-destruction but strategic sacrifice—like a farmer who plants seed in the ground, giving up immediate use to gain eventual harvest.

What might need to be laid down? Comfort zones that limit growth and service. Material security and over-dependence on possessions. Social approval from people whose values oppose God's values. Personal rights and insistence on having your own way. Future control and attempts to guarantee outcomes.

Everything we've learned about being reliable messengers creates the foundation for experiencing and demonstrating the extraordinary life Jesus offers. When people observe reliable messengers who gather consistently, grow intentionally, go sacrificially, give generously, lead through service, live with gratitude, and partner faithfully, they see evidence of life that's qualitatively different from ordinary existence.

When you experience the abundant life Jesus offers, it naturally overflows to others, creating opportunities for them to encounter the same transformation. Your extraordinary life encourages others to seek their own encounter, experience His presence, exchange their limitations, endeavor in faithful service, and encourage others to begin their transformational journey.

While abundant life is God's gift, not human achievement, it's sustained through consistent spiritual practices that maintain your connection to the source. Essential disciplines include Scripture engagement, prayer communion, worship participation, community involvement, service expression, and witness sharing.

Jesus warned that His followers would face tribulation in the world, yet He also promised abundant life. An extraordinary life doesn't eliminate difficulties but transforms how you experience and respond to them.

Like Elisabeth Elliot finding purpose and joy while serving among those who had caused her great pain, the extraordinary life finds meaning in suffering, grows through challenges, and demonstrates that God's grace is sufficient for every circumstance.

While abundant life begins now, it extends into eternity. The transformations you experience, the relationships you build, the service you provide, and the people you influence all have eternal significance that continues beyond physical death.

While each person must personally encounter Christ and experience transformation, the extraordinary life is fully realized only in community with other believers who share the same abundant life. The local church becomes the context where extraordinary life is nurtured, expressed, and multiplied.

Jesus' promise of abundant life wasn't limited to His original disciples or to specially called individuals. It's His desire and provision for every person who believes in Him. This means you don't have to settle for ordinary existence. You can experience the extraordinary life of purpose, significance, joy, and eternal impact.

While the abundant life is God's gift, experiencing it requires ongoing choices to trust His promises, obey His commands, and participate in His purposes rather than defaulting to ordinary patterns. These choices become easier with practice, but they never become automatic.

Living It Out

Reflection Questions:

1. How would you describe your current experience of life—ordinary survival or extraordinary abundance?

2. What aspects of "ordinary" life might God be calling you to lay down in order to experience the "extraordinary" life He offers?

3. How does your life demonstrate to others that following Christ leads to abundant, meaningful existence?

Weekly Challenge: Make one specific choice this week that moves you toward the extraordinary life Jesus offers. Whether it's stepping out in faith, serving someone sacrificially, or trusting God with an uncertain situation, choose abundance over ordinary existence.

Implementation Ideas:

• Evaluate your current life patterns to identify areas where you're settling for ordinary existence.

• Look for opportunities to demonstrate the joy, peace, and purpose that come from following Christ.

• Consider how your choices and lifestyle provide evidence of the extraordinary life to others.

• Remember that the extraordinary life is sustained by consistent spiritual disciplines and community relationships.

WEEK 52

COMMISSIONED AND SENT

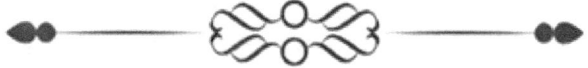

Mark 16:15-16 (ESV) - And he said to them, "Go into all the world and proclaim the gospel to the whole creation. Whoever believes and is baptized will be saved, but whoever does not believe will be condemned."

William Carey sat in a cramped ship's cabin in 1804, sailing toward India with his wife and children. Friends had called him foolish for leaving his comfortable life as a shoemaker to become a missionary to a foreign land where he didn't speak the language, understand the culture, or have any guarantee of success. Yet Carey had been gripped by Christ's simple but profound command: "Go into all the world and proclaim the gospel." What seemed like an impossible mission to others became the driving passion of his life. Carey would spend 41 years in India, translate the Bible into multiple languages, establish churches, and become known as the "Father of Modern Missions." His secret wasn't extraordinary ability but extraordinary obedience to an extraordinary commission.

As we conclude this 52-week journey of becoming reliable messengers, we return to where it all began—with Jesus' commission that transforms ordinary believers into world-changing messengers.

"Go into all the world and proclaim the gospel to the whole creation." Unlike the Matthew account which mentions "all nations," Mark emphasizes "the whole creation"—every person, in every place, deserves to hear the gospel message.

This universal scope means no one is beyond the reach of God's love or outside the responsibility of His messengers. The gospel isn't limited by geography, culture, language, or social barriers. Every reliable messenger has a role in this worldwide mission, whether through going personally or supporting those who go.

"Proclaim the gospel." The word "proclaim" (*kerysso*) means to herald or announce with authority, like a town crier delivering an official message from the king. Reliable messengers don't share opinions or suggestions—they proclaim the authoritative good news of Jesus Christ.

This proclamation includes everything we've learned about effective communication: it must be explicit (clear about sin, salvation, and response), explainable (understandable to diverse audiences), and essential (addressing humanity's greatest need for reconciliation with God).

"Whoever believes and is baptized will be saved, but whoever does not believe will be condemned." The stakes couldn't be higher—eternal salvation or eternal condemnation depends on how people respond to the gospel message reliable messengers proclaim.

This eternal significance elevates the importance of being faithful messengers. We're not just sharing helpful information or good advice—we're carrying the message that determines where people spend eternity.

The Great Commission summarizes everything we've learned about being reliable messengers. From the paradigm shifts, you can't fulfill the Great Commission while living an ordinary, comfortable, status-quo existence. From the E5

Process, making disciples requires helping people through encounter, experience, exchange, endeavor, and encouragement. From the MVVS framework, the Great Commission IS the mission—GATHER, GROW, and GO work together to create disciples who can make disciples.

The Great Commission requires both individual commitment and corporate coordination. While each believer is personally commissioned to proclaim the gospel, fulfilling this mission globally requires coordinated effort through local churches and mission organizations.

The urgency of Mark's account doesn't diminish the generational nature of this mission. Every person you help become a believer may influence hundreds or thousands of others across subsequent generations through their own gospel proclamation.

While humanitarian efforts to meet physical needs are important and commanded, the Great Commission addresses humanity's ultimate need—salvation from sin and eternal condemnation through faith in Jesus Christ.

The urgency in Mark's account reflects the ongoing nature of this mission. Each generation must take responsibility for reaching their contemporaries while also preparing future generations to continue proclaiming the gospel.

Every believer who takes the Great Commission seriously experiences the transformation we've studied throughout this year. You can't effectively proclaim the gospel without becoming the kind of person whose life validates the message— a reliable messenger who demonstrates the salvation and transformation the gospel offers.

This isn't a temporary assignment or optional activity for

those with special interest in missions. It's the defining purpose that should characterize every believer's life until death or Christ's return.

Despite opposition, setbacks, and apparent failures, the gospel will be proclaimed to the whole creation because Christ has commissioned His people to do it. Revelation 7:9 shows the ultimate result: "A great multitude which no one could number, of all nations, tribes, peoples, and tongues, standing before the throne."

This confidence motivates faithful proclamation regardless of immediate results and provides hope during difficult circumstances. You're participating in a mission that's guaranteed to succeed, even when individual efforts seem unsuccessful.

Living It Out

Reflection Questions:

1. How has this year-long study changed your understanding of what it means to be a reliable messenger?

2. What specific aspects of gospel proclamation is God calling you to focus on in the coming year?

3. How will you apply what you've learned to become more effective in proclaiming the gospel and making disciples?

Weekly Challenge: As you conclude this 52-week journey, make specific commitments about how you will live as a reliable messenger in the year ahead. Consider your role in proclaiming the gospel both locally and globally.

Implementation Ideas:

- Review the key concepts from this year-long study and identify areas where you've grown and areas needing continued development.

- Create a personal action plan for applying what you've learned about being a reliable messenger.

- Look for ways to share these concepts with others who could benefit from understanding their calling as reliable messengers.

- Remember that being commissioned and sent is not the end of your journey but the beginning of a lifetime of faithful service in proclaiming the gospel to the whole creation.

CONCLUSION

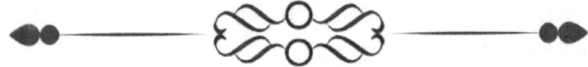

Bringing It All Together: Your Journey as a Reliable Messenger

This 52-week journey has taken you from understanding what makes a messenger reliable to living as a commissioned representative of Jesus Christ. You've discovered that God has both called and equipped you to be His reliable messenger, not because you're perfect but because you're available to His transforming work.

The paradigm shifts from anchors to oars, cruise ship to fishing boat, fear to freedom, and parishioner to practitioner have prepared you for active participation in God's mission. The E5 process has shown you how encounter, experience, exchange, endeavor, and encouragement create transformation that reproduces itself in others.

The church's MVVS framework provides practical structure for living as a reliable messenger through gathering, growing, and going while learning, loving, and living God's Word. The T4 stewardship of time, talents, treasures, and testimony gives you concrete ways to invest your life for maximum kingdom impact.

Through biblical examples and practical application, you've learned that being a reliable messenger isn't about perfection but about faithfulness. It's not about having all the answers but about sharing what you've experienced. And it's not about being extraordinary but about letting God work extraordinarily through ordinary people who make themselves available to His purposes.

Here's what I hope you'll remember: as you continue this journey beyond these 52 weeks, being a reliable messenger is both a calling and a process. You'll continue growing in understanding and effectiveness as you remain faithful to the principles and practices you've learned. Most importantly, you'll discover that the abundant life Jesus promised comes not from pursuing your own dreams but from participating in His eternal purposes as a reliable messenger of His grace and truth.

The world desperately needs reliable messengers who can bridge the gap between divine truth and human need. You have been equipped for this calling. Now go forth as a reliable messenger, commissioned and sent by the One who has all authority in heaven and earth, confident in His promise to be with you always, even to the end of the age.

RESOURCES

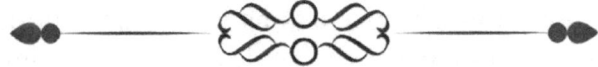

A Note to the Reader: The stories in this guide have been drawn from a variety of sources to illustrate timeless principles about being God's reliable messenger. For those interested in learning more about the historical figures and events mentioned, the following resources provide deeper exploration.

Historical Accounts - Books and Primary Sources

Week 1: Ruby Bridges - *Through My Eyes* by Ruby Bridges (Scholastic Press, 1999)

Week 2: Gladys Aylward - *The Small Woman* by Alan Burgess (Evans Brothers, 1957); *Gladys Aylward: The Little Woman* by Gladys Aylward with Christine Hunter (Moody Press, 1970)

Week 3: Dietrich Bonhoeffer - *Bonhoeffer: Pastor, Martyr, Prophet, Spy* by Eric Metaxas (Thomas Nelson, 2010)

Week 6: John F. Kennedy (Moon Landing Goal) - *JFK and the Race to the Moon* by John M. Logsdon (Palgrave Macmillan, 2010)

Week 8: Corrie ten Boom - *The Hiding Place* by Corrie ten Boom with John and Elizabeth Sherrill (Chosen Books, 1971); *Tramp for the Lord* by Corrie ten Boom (Christian Literature Crusade, 1974)

Week 9: Hudson Taylor - *Hudson Taylor's Spiritual Secret* by Dr. and Mrs. Howard Taylor (Moody Press, 1932); *Hudson*

Taylor: Deep in the Heart of China by Janet and Geoff Benge (YWAM Publishing, 1998)

Week 10: William Carey - *William Carey: Obliged to Go* by Janet and Geoff Benge (YWAM Publishing, 1998); *The Life and Letters of William Carey* by George Smith (1885, various modern reprints)

Week 12: Brother Lawrence - *The Practice of the Presence of God* by Brother Lawrence (various editions, originally published posthumously in 1692 from his letters and conversations)

Week 13: George Müller - *George Müller: The Guardian of Bristol's Orphans* by Janet and Geoff Benge (YWAM Publishing, 1999); *Autobiography of George Müller* by George Müller (originally published 1899, various modern editions)

Week 14: Rosa Parks - *Rosa Parks: My Story* by Rosa Parks with Jim Haskins (Dial Books, 1992); *Quiet Strength: The Faith, the Hope, and the Heart of a Woman Who Changed a Nation* by Rosa Parks (Zondervan, 1994)

Week 16: King George VI - *The King's Speech: How One Man Saved the British Monarchy* by Mark Logue and Peter Conradi (Sterling, 2010)

Week 17: Alexander Graham Bell - *The Telephone Gambit* by Seth Shulman (W. W. Norton & Company, 2008)

Week 18: Martin Luther King Jr. - *Letter from Birmingham Jail* by Martin Luther King Jr. (1963); *Why We Can't Wait* by Martin Luther King Jr. (Signet Classics, 2000)

Week 19: George W. Bush (9/11 response) - *Decision Points* by George W. Bush (Crown Publishers, 2010)

Week 20: Winston Churchill - *The Second World War* (six volumes) by Winston Churchill (Houghton Mifflin, 1948-1953)

Week 23: John Frank Stevens - *The Path Between the Seas* by David McCullough (Simon & Schuster, 1977)

Week 25: Klaus Fuchs - *Klaus Fuchs: The Man Who Stole the Atom Bomb* by Norman Moss (Grafton, 1987)

Week 26: Raphael and Pietro Perugino - *Raphael: His Life and Works* by Julia Cartwright (1895, various modern reprints)

Week 27: Henry Ford - *My Life and Work* by Henry Ford with Samuel Crowther (1922, various modern reprints)

Week 28: Etty Hillesum - *An Interrupted Life: The Diaries of Etty Hillesum* (Pantheon Books, 1983)

Week 29: George Washington Carver - *George Washington Carver: His Life & Faith in His Own Words* by William J. Federer (Amerisearch, 2002)

Week 30: Paul Brand - *The Gift of Pain* by Paul Brand and Philip Yancey (Zondervan, 1997)

Week 31: Guglielmo Marconi - *Marconi: The Man Who Networked the World* by Marc Raboy (Oxford University Press, 2016); *My Father, Marconi* by Degna Marconi (Guernica Editions, 1982)

Week 32: Louis Zamperini - *Unbroken* by Laura Hillenbrand (Random House, 2010); *Devil at My Heels* by Louis Zamperini (William Morrow, 2003)

Week 33: John Glenn - *John Glenn: A Memoir* by John Glenn with Nick Taylor (Bantam Books, 1999)

Week 34: Martin Luther - *Here I Stand: A Life of Martin Luther* by Roland Bainton (Abingdon Press, 1950)

Week 35: Alexander Fleming - *Alexander Fleming: The Man and the Myth* by Gwyn Macfarlane (Harvard University Press, 1984)

Week 36: Edmund Hillary and Tenzing Norgay - *High Adventure* by Edmund Hillary (Hodder & Stoughton, 1955); *View from the Summit* by Edmund Hillary (Doubleday, 1999); *Tiger of the Snows* by Tenzing Norgay with James Ramsey Ullman (Putnam, 1955)

Week 37: Howard Schultz/Starbucks - *Pour Your Heart Into It* by Howard Schultz (Hyperion, 1997)

Week 38: Wright Brothers - *The Wright Brothers* by David McCullough (Simon & Schuster, 2015)

Week 39: Ray Kroc/McDonald's - *Grinding It Out: The Making of McDonald's* by Ray Kroc (Contemporary Books, 1977)

Week 40: John F. Kennedy - *JFK and the Race to the Moon* by John M. Logsdon (Palgrave Macmillan, 2010)

Week 42: Florence Nightingale - *Florence Nightingale: The Making of an Icon* by Mark Bostridge (Farrar, Straus and Giroux, 2008)

Week 43: C.T. Studd - *C.T. Studd: Cricketer and Pioneer* by Norman Grubb (Christian Literature Crusade, 1933)

Week 44: Benjamin Franklin - *The Autobiography of Benjamin Franklin* (various editions, originally published posthumously); *Poor Richard's Almanack* by Benjamin Franklin (originally published 1732-1758, various modern compilations)

Week 45: Albert Einstein - *Einstein: His Life and Universe* by Walter Isaacson (Simon & Schuster, 2007)

Week 46: John D. Rockefeller - *Titan: The Life of John D. Rockefeller, Sr.* by Ron Chernow (Random House, 1998)

Week 47: Greensboro Sit-ins - *The Sit-Ins: Protest and Legal Change in the Civil Rights Era* by Christopher W. Schmidt (University of Chicago Press, 2018)

Week 48: Johnson & Johnson Tylenol Crisis - *The Tylenol Mafia* by Scott Bartz (Barricade Books, 2012)

Week 49: Robert F. Kennedy - *Make Gentle the Life of This World: The Vision of Robert F. Kennedy* edited by Maxwell Taylor Kennedy (Harcourt Brace, 1998)

Week 51: Elisabeth Elliot - *Through Gates of Splendor* by Elisabeth Elliot (Tyndale House, 1957); *The Savage My Kinsman* by Elisabeth Elliot (Servant Publications, 1961)

Week 52: William Carey - *William Carey: Obliged to Go* by Janet and Geoff Benge (YWAM Publishing, 1998)

Stories Inspired by True Events

These stories are based on historical events but include reconstructed dialogue or details:

- Wright Brothers' approach to teaching aviation
- World War II radio operators and air raid wardens
- Hernán Cortés and the burning of ships
- Marine training methods during WWII
- Titanic and its focus on luxury

- London Blitz underground communities

Teaching Illustrations

These are narratives or modern parables created to illustrate spiritual principles:

- Maria's transformation from parishioner to practitioner

- David Thompson's hospital in Cameroon (representative missionary story)

Additional Recommended Reading

On Being a Reliable Messenger:

- *The Master Plan of Evangelism* by Robert E. Coleman

- *Spiritual Leadership* by J. Oswald Sanders

- *Transforming Discipleship* by Greg Ogden

On Spiritual Formation:

- *The Spirit of the Disciplines* by Dallas Willard

- *Celebration of Discipline* by Richard Foster

- *The Practice of the Presence of God* by Brother Lawrence

On Mission and Ministry:

- *Let the Nations Be Glad!* by John Piper

- *The Forgotten Ways* by Alan Hirsch

- *When Helping Hurts* by Steve Corbett and Brian Fikkert

May these resources enrich your continued journey as a reliable messenger of God's grace and truth.

Made in the USA
Columbia, SC
20 January 2026

77742780R00137